WONDERS

Without Number

Created with Purpose, or Conceived from Chaos?

DAVID RIVES

Wonders Without Number

Created with Purpose, or Conceived from Chaos?

ISBN: 978-0-9857926-3-3
Printed in the United States of America
Third Printing, March 2015

P.O. BOX 2824 - LEWISBURG, TN 37091
info@davidrivesministries.org
Visit our website at www.davidrives.com

TABLE OF CONTENTS

ACKNOWLEDGEMENTS

The author would like to thank
Family and friends who pushed me to excel.
My parents, for raising me in God's love.
My brother, for always being there.

I would also like to thank the readers, who have made my dreams a reality by your support and encouragement.

Most of all, I would like to thank the Creator of heaven and Earth, my Savior, Yeshua of Nazareth, Jesus Christ. This book is dedicated to proclaiming ***His glory****.*

TEXTUAL CONSIDERATIONS

The English translation of Biblical text quoted in this book is that of the King James Version (KJV).

When a more in depth understanding of scripture is necessary the "Masoretic Hebrew Text" and the "Received Greek Text" are used.

King James translators chose the word "God" spelled with a capital "G" for the New Testament representation of the Biblical God (יהוה YHWH), (אלהים ELOHIM).

"In the beginning God (אלהים Elohim) *created the heaven and the earth."*

FOREWORD

By Dr. Danny Faulkner

Evolution is the great creation myth of our time. There are many misconceptions about evolution. A common misconception is that evolution is concerned solely with biology. That is, that evolution is the development of living organisms over time. Many people even want to separate a naturalistic origin of life from biological evolution. However, at its core, evolution is a commitment to explain the world around us entirely in terms of natural processes. Hence, it makes no sense to speak of the natural development of life over time if one does not also accept the proposition that life arose without Divine intervention. Furthermore, evolution has permeated nearly all areas of human thought. Hence, we can speak of three broad categories of evolution: cosmological, geological, and biological.

Another common misconception is that belief in evolution and biblical creation are compatible. However, if the world around us came about in an entirely natural way, then there is no need for a Creator. On the other hand, if God created us and the world around us in the manner described in Genesis, then there is no need to appeal to naturalistic theories of the origin of the world. Nor is there any place in the biblical text for naturalistic processes, for the Bible tells us that God created everything in six normal days and that the creation was just a few thousand years ago. Evolution requires vast amounts of time. Most scientists today believe that the world is billions of years old, but that belief primarily is based upon a commitment to evolution rather than real data.

There are many other books about creation, so why publish one more? In this book, David Rives introduces his Rives theory of relativity: "If your relatives can't understand what you are talking about, you need to use simpler terms!" That's good advice. The author applies this theory while tackling a broad range of topics. These topics include the origin of the universe, the origin of the earth, the origin of life, and the origin of man. A thorough discussion of any of these topics would fill books much larger than this one. However, this book isn't meant to be a thorough treatment. Rather, it is an introduction to the creation/evolution debate that nearly everyone's relatives can understand. David Rives is an accomplished speaker, and he brings to his writing the same clear style that he employs in his speaking.

While Mr. Rives is not a scientist, he does understand the issues very well. As an accomplished amateur astronomer, he has done some stunning astrophotography. A little of his work is included in illustrations in this book. I look forward to more of his astrophotography.

Mr. Rives has worked in some other interesting items as well. For instance, he briefly describes the background of some of the people instrumental in our understanding of astronomy and some of the people involved in developing evolutionary ideas. The book contains some lore about the constellations and stars. There even are some star charts to help the reader look for some of the things discussed in this book. David Rives further develops his Rives theory of relativity to illustrate the vast distances that we encounter in astronomy.

This is a book about creation, and even more importantly, our Creator. You will find many biblical passages within the pages of this book. If you come away from this book with one single thing, it is the sincere prayer of the author and of me that this one thing be a salvation experience with Jesus Christ. You see, nothing else in this life matters as much as this.

Danny R. Faulkner
Astronomer, Answers in Genesis

Distinguished Professor Emeritus, the University of South Carolina Lancaster

The Rosette Nebula - Caldwell 49
Photo by David Rives
The Rosette Nebula, as imaged by David Rives Ministries telescopes, reveals an astonishing rose-shaped cloud of gas in the constellation Monoceros.

PREFACE

As we witness the indescribable beauty of our Creator's Universe and consider the wonders of His Creation, we begin to understand that empirical science, things that can be proven scientifically, in no way contradicts the words of scripture.

In contrast to what evolutionary science teaches, we are not highly developed animals, the product of random chance. Just as the heavens and earth were carefully designed, *we* are "fearfully and wonderfully made" by a loving God.

My study of Creation science and astronomy, along with my work in the field of Biblical archaeology, *all point to the validity* of the Biblical record and proclaim the glory of God. By way of this book, I hope to leave readers with renewed confidence in the literal Word of God. From Genesis through Revelation, from the time of Creation to the New Heavens and Earth, the Bible is the history of the world *and* our handbook for life. We learn of our purpose on Earth and of our need of a Savior to deliver us from sin and death. The Creation account as described in the book of Genesis was a literal event, and the sin committed by Adam and Eve in the garden was just as real. Only by way of a literal understanding of the book of Genesis can a person begin to understand that the result of sin is death, and that the reason Jesus Christ came to Earth was to present us with the opportunity for a solution. Forgiveness of sin and eternal life is available for all those who receive Him as their Savior.

Will we believe the words of scripture and face contempt from theoretical science, or will we conform our beliefs to the worldly views of evolution and the idea that there is no such thing as moral absolutes? In a world of compromise, many choose the latter, attempting to conform Biblical truths to the theories of men.

The intended purpose of this book is twofold: To leave Christian readers with a renewed interest in scripture; and to leave the unbelieving reader with a hunger to seek the Creator for answers in order to be saved. I hope to leave you with information that is not only relevant, but extremely important in this day and time - the tools you need to combat the dangerous and false theories of Darwinian and cosmic evolution.

Whether you are seeking answers to questions about the accuracy of the Bible as compared to secular science, or if you simply want to be encouraged in your love of the Bible, hopefully this book will enlighten and inspire, as it takes you on a journey through the wonders of the universe... *Wonders Without Number.*

If, by way of this book, I can encourage you in your walk with Christ and strengthen your faith, then I will feel it has been a success.

If, by way of this book, I can help to lead others to a belief in the Word of God and the acceptance of Yeshua of Nazareth, Jesus Christ, as their Savior, then *not only I, but the Angels of God, will be filled with joy.*

"I say unto you, that likewise joy shall be in heaven over one sinner that repenteth, more than over ninety and nine just persons, which need no repentance." ...Luke 15:7

The Great Orion Nebula - Messier 42, M42, or NGC 1976
Photo by David Rives
The Orion Nebula is one of the brightest nebulae visible to the naked eye. The diffuse nebula is located below the belt stars in the constellation Orion and is located approximately 1300 light years from Earth. The nebula is estimated to be 24 light years across.

Chapter One
A Story of Beginnings

David Rives with the 16" Mobile Observatory Telescope

In 2007, David Rives Ministries began as an idea, a vision of using astronomy and Creation science as a means to share the truths of scripture, a way to present the Gospel—the good news about our Creator and Savior, *Jesus Christ, Yeshua of Nazareth.*

The Holy Bible contains an historical record of the world from the time of Creation. In addition, it contains a prophetic guideline as to future events and the destiny of mankind. That record begins in the book of Genesis, which in the Greek language means "origins".

In its original Hebrew it is known as *B'reshit* or "beginning". In the very first sentence and the foundation of the whole Bible, we learn that "*In the beginning, God created the heaven and the earth*". So let's start at the VERY beginning.

> בראשית ברא אלהים
> את השמים ואת הארץ:
>
> ***—Genesis 1:1***

There are many different ideas about what took place *in the beginning.* On one hand, we have the Biblical record. On the other hand, we have a number of unproven theories. From the plain language of scripture, it is easy to learn what the Bible has to say. Let us consider what the Word of God relates in comparison to the theoretical words of men.

And God saw every thing that he had made, and, behold, it was very good.

—Genesis 1:31

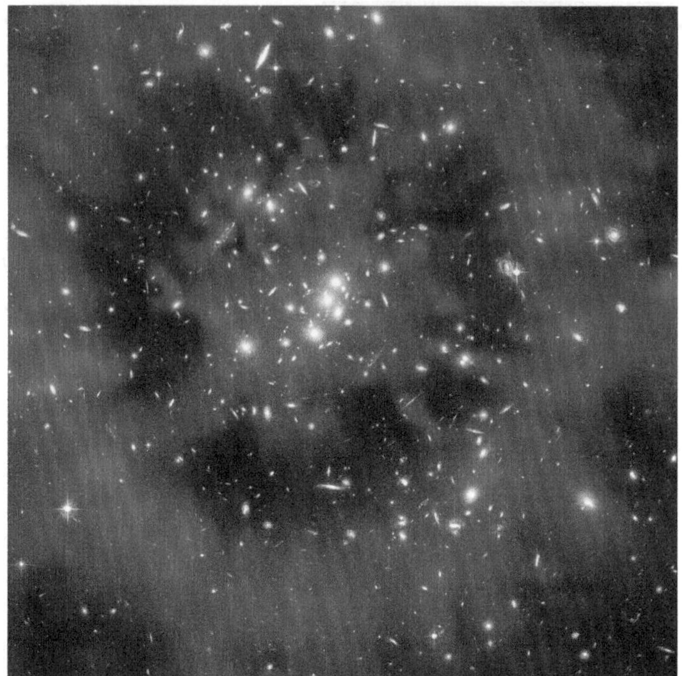

Galaxy Cluster CL0024+17 taken by the Hubble Space Telescope Located in the constellation Pisces, the elongated streaks of light are distant galaxies. It is thought that what we see is somewhat distorted due to an effect called gravitational lensing.

THE BIBLICAL ACCOUNT VS THE IMAGINATIONS OF MEN

The Bible tells us that in six days God created the Sun, the Moon, the stars, and everything that we see around us, including mankind. However, there are those who propose alternative views such as the theory of cosmic evolution (beginning with a big bang), and the theory of Darwinian evolution, the idea that organisms arise by means of natural selection.

Let us examine evolutionary cosmology, or cosmic evolution, a Creation account directly opposed to that which we find in the book of Genesis—*The Book of Beginnings.*

Cosmic evolutionists state that around 14 billion years ago, the Universe suddenly appeared in an expanding state, and that this expansion, carrying matter with it, has continued since. Supposedly, over long periods of time, this matter somehow came together and formed everything we see around us. This theory, taught as fact by many, has become known as the "Big Bang theory".

One of the inherent problems with the Big Bang theory is that it doesn't explain the origin of the Universe. It only theorizes how the Universe took on its current shape.

THE BIG BANG

What was it?
Who lit the fuse?

You cannot have a Big Bang without enormous amounts of matter. So where did the matter come from? Has it always existed? What is the purpose of its existence, and how did it come to be? No satisfactory answers have ever been given to these questions from an atheistic perspective, which leaves us with the possibility of Creation by a Creator. While some search for an entirely natural explanation to the Universe, the mere EXISTENCE of matter suggests design.

"Wishing don't make it so."

Today, many accept the Big Bang theory as fact simply because it is a popular theory that has been accepted by their peers. It is a theory that is being presented as if everyone is supposed to believe it. Most never stop to consider the fact that, in the past, many popular theories have been proven to be false. Theories that people really wanted to be true were superseded by newer theories.

FLAT EARTH THEORY:

Many ancient cultures believed that the surface of the Earth was a flat plane, possibly floating on water. The long-held theory of the flat Earth was replaced with that of a spherical Earth when empirical scientific data was presented. It is a popular misconception among those educated in the U.S. that Christopher Columbus was the first to dispel such a notion. Certainly the spherical shape of the Earth was proposed long before, in ancient Greece.

The Flat Earth theory as represented in an 1800's wood engraving

The Black Death as depicted in Pieter Bruegel's "Triumph of Death"

MIASMA THEORY:

The Miasma theory was the idea that diseases, including the Black Death, were caused by poisonous air. When the discoveries made by Louis Pasteur pointed away from the Miasma theory, it was replaced with the Germ theory. In spite of the improbable nature of the Miasma theory and the evidence provided by Pasteur, the transition to the Germ theory was difficult for many to accept.

"The Black Death" claimed almost one half of Europe's population, and was one of the most devastating pandemics in recorded history.

STEADY STATE THEORY:

The Steady State theory indicated that although the Universe is expanding, matter is constantly produced from nowhere, making the cosmos always appear full. For the most part, this odd theory has been replaced by another theory with almost as many problems: the Big Bang theory.

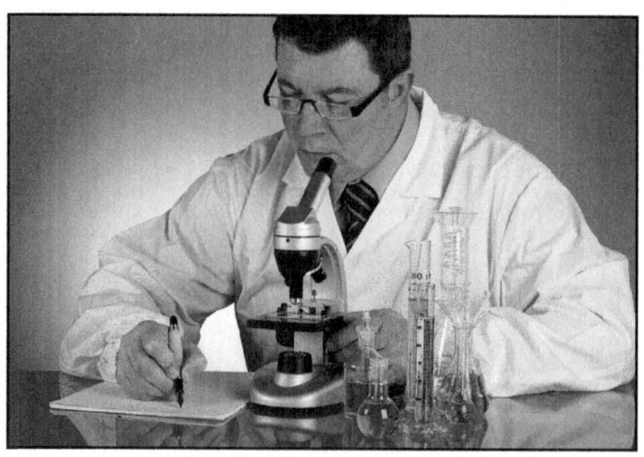

SCIENTIFIC METHOD

True scientific method requires more than the formation of a hypothesis. It involves the testing of ideas—empirical data which can be demonstrated. Observations must be duplicated in order to determine the plausibility of a theory.

Empirical data helps us discover the problems or strengths of a hypothesis through experimentation.

Today, many would tell us that the Biblical account of Creation as recorded by Moses is only a theory. They claim that no one was around to witness the event. Those of us who believe the Bible would not agree. Yes, someone was around to witness the event of Creation—the Creator Himself.

The book of John tells us that Yeshua, Jesus Christ was the Creator. Questioning the leaders of His day, Jesus asked, *"Had ye believed Moses, ye would have believed me: for he wrote of me. But if ye believe not his writings, how shall ye believe my words?"*

The words of Jesus confirm the writings of Moses, including the book of Genesis. They make it plain that what we see around us was not the result of natural selection. In six days He created all things, including mankind—*at the beginning He made them male and female.* If we believe the Bible, then we have an historical account that is based on the words of the Creator Himself.

BIBLICAL EXEGESIS

Today, exegesis is a major component of theological training. The word "exegesis" is derived from a Greek word which means "to lead". We have to be careful because it involves man's interpretation of scripture, and there is a fine line between Exegesis and Eisegesis, reading one's own ideas into the text.

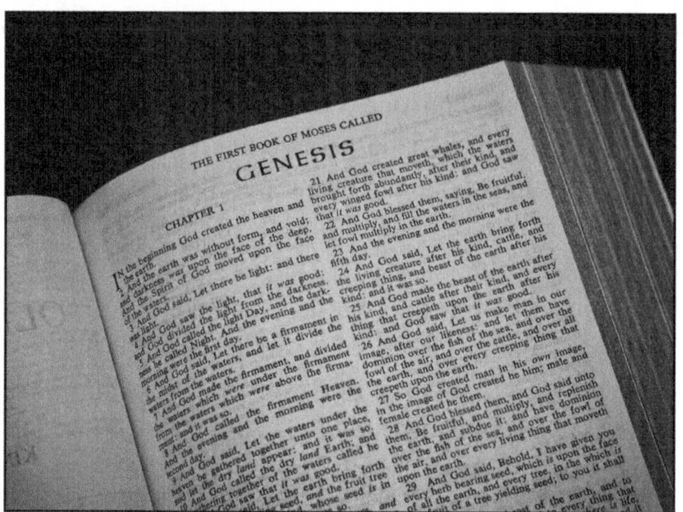

The Bible tells us plainly that *in the beginning, God created the heaven and earth in six days.* That is what I believe, and because of that, I am often criticized. Many Christians have been educated in schools and universities steeped in evolutionary science. Some tell me that if only I would use Biblical Exegesis more properly, we would all come to understand that the Creation account can't be taken literally.

WHY DO CHRISTIANS COMPROMISE?

Why should we settle for a stretched interpretation of scripture in order to conform to unproven theories of evolution?

The Bible warns of those who try to add to the scriptures; yet, today, many teachers add their own ideas in order to explain things in a way that fits <u>their theology.</u>

As if that is not bad enough, some scholars attempt to rationalize their beliefs through metaphysical rambling—and in metaphysics, the imagination is the limit. Colossians warns: *"Beware lest any man spoil you through philosophy and vain deceit...."* The word translated *"spoil"* in the Greek means "to lead you away," and today, many have been lead away by blind leaders professing themselves to be wise.

Every passage in the Bible should first and foremost be looked at simply and in context. It was written so that almost everyone can understand, not in such a way that allows only brilliant minds to interpret it.

We must not settle for a Biblical interpretation which *conforms* to current scientific thought. We should insist on using the WORD OF GOD as our foundation for science. His *word is true—from the beginning.*

"...Beware lest ye also, being led away with the error of the wicked, fall from your own stedfastness."
—2 Peter 3:17

COMPROMISE
IS NOT THE ANSWER

Chapter Two

The Big Bang and Science

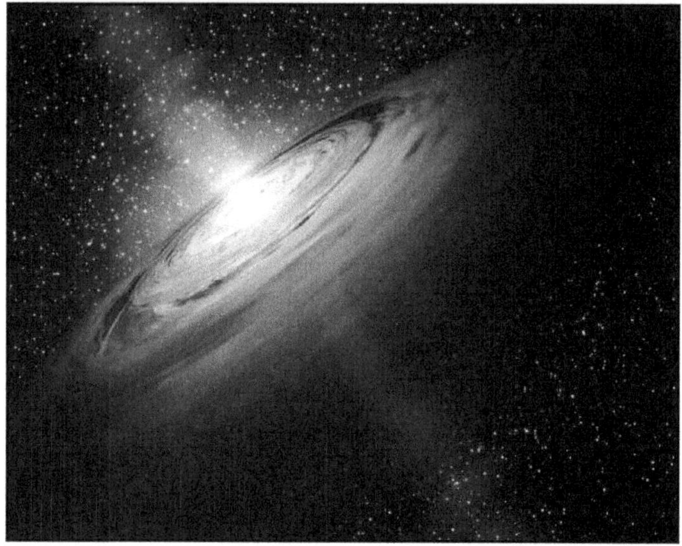

The Genesis account of Creation states that God formed *the heaven and the earth* in *six days*. Modern science gives us a contradictory view, cutting God out of the equation entirely. Some theorize that around 14 billion years ago, the Universe suddenly appeared and that this eventually caused everything we see around us to form. This idea is commonly known as the Big Bang theory.

One of the inherent problems with the Big Bang theory is that it doesn't explain the origin of the Universe. It only theorizes how the Universe took on its current shape.

The respected Harvard-Smithsonian Center for Astrophysics asks "Where did all the stuff in the universe come from in the first place?" They don't propose an answer because science has none. The Bible, on the other hand, gives a simple, easy to understand explanation: In the beginning, God created it.

NASA's VIEW:
"Although the Big Bang Theory is widely accepted, it probably will never be proved; consequentially, leaving a number of tough, unanswered questions."

While NASA is aware of the many difficulties with the current accepted theories, the models used in study of the cosmos are still almost all based on the Big Bang. Many people have trouble accepting that not everything can be explained by naturalism. They might point out that "*at this time*" some things cannot be explained naturally but will be uncovered in the future. The future will indeed bring more knowledge, as has been the case since the beginning. But what if that increased knowledge only serves to confirm the necessity of a Creator? We cannot be blind to facts, whatever they may be, and should always be willing to study a matter for ourselves. In science, new theories have to be compatible to existing scientific laws to uphold their status as a legitimate theory. As a Christian, I believe the Bible should stand as our unalterable law, and new theories should be fully compatible with it before being accepted.

Will we believe the words of scripture, or will we accept non-Biblical theory as fact? Let us heed the words of King David, *"It is better to trust in the LORD than to put confidence in man." —Psalm 118:8*

WHERE'S THE HEAVY METAL

The Big Bang is supposed to have produced the basic elements hydrogen and helium, and from these two, all of the elements that make up the periodic table were supposedly formed. This is a grand theory, but has never been demonstrated or observed. Here is what we do know about the basic elements:

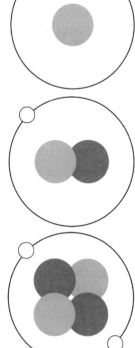

Shown on right, hydrogen (MASS 1) is composed of one electron and one proton.

Deuterium, (MASS 2) is an isotope of hydrogen. It is composed of one electron, one proton, and one neutron.

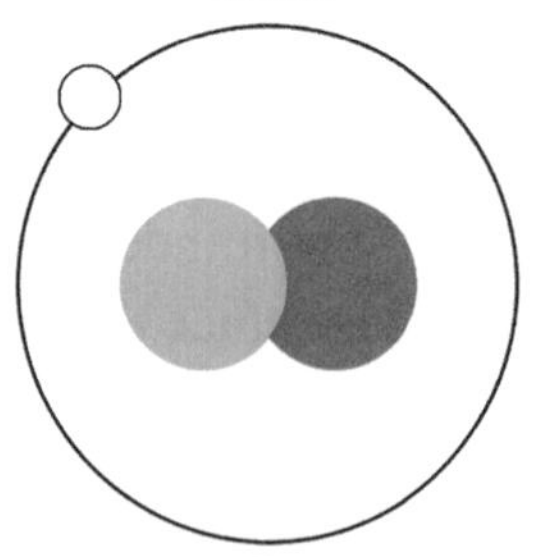

By way of nuclear fusion, it is possible to take deuterium and produce helium (MASS 4).

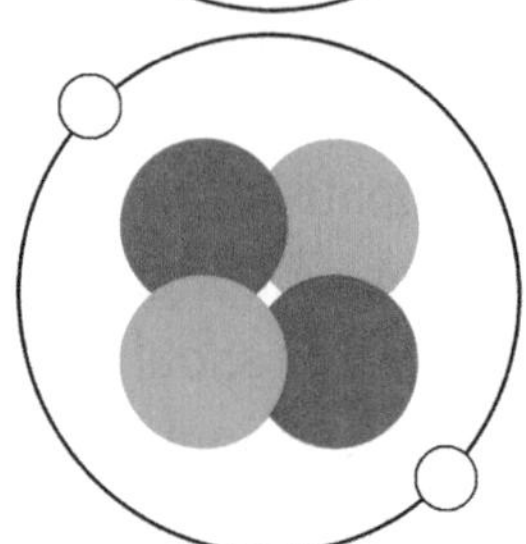

One might assume that this process of taking simple elements and producing heavier elements could continue on indefinitely. That, however, would be a big assumption, as the process has never been observed in nature. In fact, there are bottlenecks in the chain of stable elements more massive than helium that would theoretically cause the production of heavy elements to come to a halt.

So where did the heavy metal come from? The Bible tells us that in the beginning God created the heaven, the Earth, and everything—all the elements on the periodic table. He did it in six days, and *it was good.*

MATTER RACING OUTWARD

Big Bang proponents tell us that around 14 billion years ago, all matter began an extremely quick expansion and eventually formed the Universe in it's current state. They cannot begin to tell us how the matter got there in the first place. According to some scientists, immediately after the "Big Bang," matter began racing outward.

Many would lead us to believe that at some non-specific point gravity began to attract the particles of matter, eventually forming shapes such as nebulae.

On the surface, that may sound very good, but there are some very important facts that they leave out. There would be no way to unite the particles. In frictionless, empty space, the particles would continue to move away from each other at a rapid pace and never slow down. Based on current scientific principles, they could not change directions and would maintain the same vector, forever becoming more separated from the rest of the matter. They would be travelling at supersonic speeds, and every second that passed would ensure that they traveled farther and farther apart, not closer together.

...Just one more example of the speculative contradictions associated with the Big Bang theory.

Supposed "Young Stars" within the Orion Nebula, forming a well-known cluster called "The Trapezium"

HOW THE STARS WERE FORMED

In a similar manner, evolutionary cosmology indicates that after the Big Bang, particles of matter came together forming clouds of gas and, subsequently, stars.

Once again, there is a BIG PROBLEM. There is no gas known to man that clumps together. It always pushes apart. It is a physical law that gas in a vacuum expands, not contracts. If you can't get gases to accumulate, there would never be enough mutual gravity to form stars. In actuality, most scientists believe that nebulae do not contain enough gas to produce stars!

ON THE FOURTH DAY

And God said, Let there be lights in the firmament of the heaven to divide the day from the night; and let them be for signs, and for seasons, and for days, and years: And let them be for lights in the firmament of the heaven to give light upon the earth: and it was so. And God made two great lights; the greater light to rule the day, and the lesser light to rule the night: he made the stars also. And God set them in the firmament of the heaven to give light upon the earth, And to rule over the day and over the night, and to divide the light from the darkness: and God saw that it was good. And the evening and the morning were the fourth day.

—Genesis 1:14-19

"Praise him, all ye stars of light.... Let them praise the name of the LORD: for he commanded, and they were created."
—Psalm 148:3-5

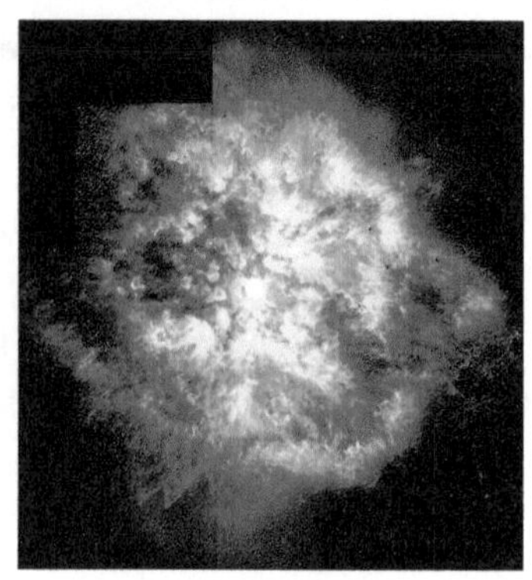

SUPERNOVAE

Scientific theory defines a supernova as a star that has reached a critical point, causing it to explode in a spectacular display of light.

Based on some versions of the Big Bang theory, shortly after a violent expansion of matter 14 billion years ago, stars began forming and later exploding. Supposedly, as the first stars went supernova, or exploded, they gave rise to a second generation of stars called Population II stars. As these went supernova, a third generation was borne. This sequence is proposed in an effort to find a means for the development of heavy elements.

It is interesting to note that we observe very little supernova activity. Very few stars are actually exploding, and there are not anywhere near enough supernovae to produce the elements that we see today. In May 2011, I was able to photograph a supernova in M51. This is a rare event, even considering that M51 is thought to contain over 200 billion stars (See following page)

Not only are exploding stars somewhat rare, astronomers cannot find first generation stars. Without the existence of these stars, second and third generation stars could not exist.

Supernova in M51 The Whirlpool Galaxy

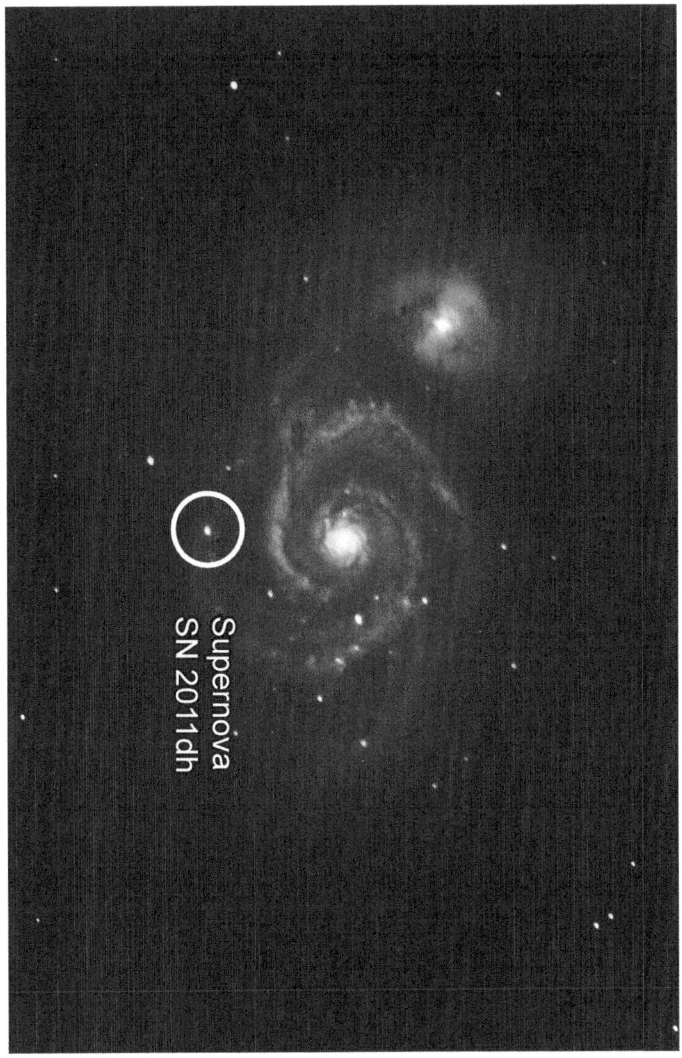

Messier 51, The Whirlpool Galaxy, taken with the David Rives Ministries Telescope. May 2011. An observable supernova (a somewhat rare event) can be seen circled in the photograph.

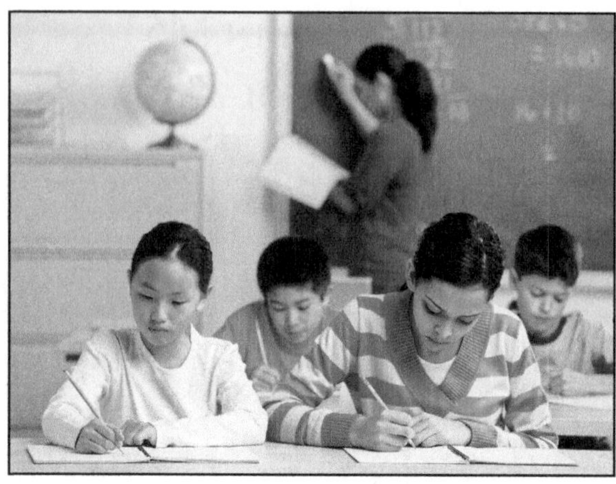

INDOCTRINATION IN SCHOOLS

Around the world, most public schools are teaching the Big Bang theory as fact. This is not only incredibly biased and one-sided, but it is an extremely dangerous concept that leads us away from the truths of Scripture found in Torah, the first books of the Bible.

One popular high school textbook states "18 to 20 billion years ago all the matter in the universe was concentrated into one very dense, very hot region that may have been much smaller than a period on this page."
Another textbook claims... "...from this state of nothingness the universe began in a gigantic explosion about 16.5 billion years ago."

In other words, nothing created everything!

It must be noted that over the past few decades the supposed age has been "refined" over and over again, and at current printing, 13.8 billion years is considered to be the *most accurate* date for the Big Bang.

In curriculum guidebooks, teachers are encouraged to "Stress that the earth is thought to be at least 4.5 billion years old." What is taking place in our schools can be described in no better way than by the term "brainwashing". What is being presented is not based on unbiased, factual science.

If we allow teachers and educators to convince impressionable young people that the first chapter of the Bible is only a failed attempt, by man, to document the history of the Universe, then how will they distinguish which parts of the Bible to believe as fact and which parts to disregard as mere fables?

What we see around us reveals order that no big bang could ever have achieved. Even so, many teachers have been led to believe that they're dealing with a form of science, and I would agree… **SCIENCE FICTION.**

A BIBLICAL BIG BANG?

Yes, there is a big bang referenced in the Bible, but <u>not the one presented by evolutionists.</u> According to the book of 2 Peter, one day *the heavens shall pass away with a GREAT NOISE.*

2 Peter 3... "Knowing this first, that there shall come in the last days scoffers, walking after their own lusts, And saying, Where is the promise of his coming? for since the fathers fell asleep, all things continue as they were from the beginning of the creation. For this they willingly are ignorant of, that by the word of God the heavens were of old, and the earth standing out of the water and in the water: Whereby the world that then was, being overflowed with water, perished: But the heavens and the earth, which are now, by the same word are kept in store, reserved unto fire against the day of judgment and perdition of ungodly men... But the day of the Lord will come as a thief in the night; in the which ***the heavens shall pass away with a great noise****, and the elements shall melt with fervent heat, the earth also and the works that are therein shall be burned up... Nevertheless we, according to his promise, look for new heavens and a new earth, wherein dwelleth righteousness."*

"Beware lest ye also, being led away with the error of the wicked, fall from your own stedfastness." —2 Peter 3

Yes, in the new heavens and the new Earth, righteousness will prevail, and no one will question the Creator.

> *"For, behold, I create new heavens and a new earth: and the former shall not be remembered, nor come into mind. But be ye glad and rejoice for ever in that which I create: for, behold, I create Jerusalem a rejoicing, and her people a joy. And I will rejoice in Jerusalem, and joy in my people: and the voice of weeping shall be no more heard in her, nor the voice of crying."*
>
> *—Isaiah 65:17-19*

Chapter Three
Is the Big Bang Biblical?

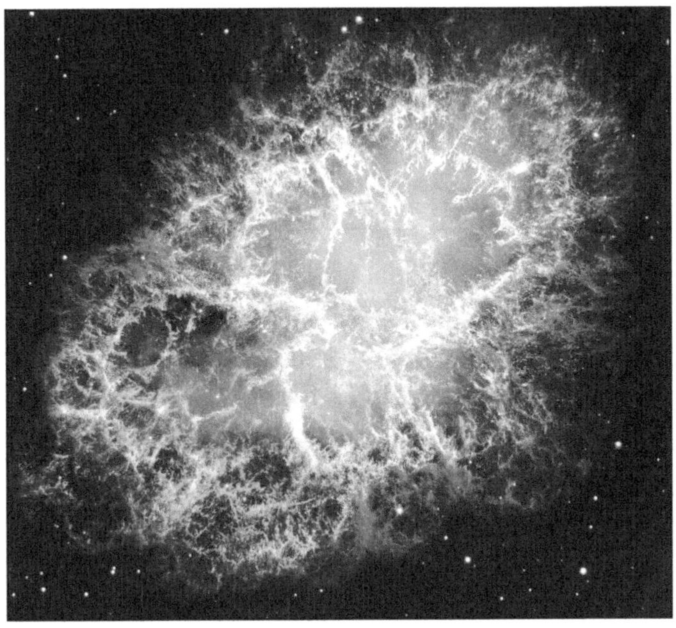

Messier 1 - The Crab Nebula, located in Taurus. Believed to be the remnants of a supernova recorded in 1054 A.D. The first object to be recorded in the Messier catalogue.

Is the Big Bang Biblical? Let us take a look at the Big Bang theory and see how it stands up to the historical record of Creation as found in the Bible.

"Let God be true, but every man a liar..."
—Romans 3:4

THE BIBLICAL RECORD	THE THEORIES OF MAN
The Bible states that *in the beginning, God created the heaven and the earth* from void, or nothing.	Some astronomers would have us believe that a Big Bang created the stars and planets.
The Bible says that God formed the material that became the Universe.	The Big Bang model disagrees, having no explanation of how the matter got there in the first place.
The Bible makes it plain that the Universe was formed within a literal week of *evenings and mornings.*	The Big Bang tells us that the universe took billions and billions of years to form.
The Bible indicates that God is the founder of the laws, such as gravity.	Evolutionists have no explanation as to how the laws came into existence, or how they work together perfectly and calculably.
The Bible says that stars were formed on day four.	The Big Bang theory indicates that matter coalesced into new stars over millions and millions of years.

The Bible says that Earth came first.	Evolutionists tell us that Earth was one of the last things to be formed.
The Bible describes the Earth as being specially formed for habitation... ...A carefully designed Universe.	Evolution indicates a chaotic, chance lottery drawing that leaves us standing here today as little more than a smarter primate.
The Bible clearly states that man was given dominion over all the animals.	Evolutionists teach us that we ARE animals.

The Big Bang theory is a God-less theory. Even if it is twisted to include a sort of God-directed big bang, it clearly calls for the dismissal of massive portions of the literal Holy Bible. This is not a direction anyone should ever purposely go. Even so, there are people narrow-minded enough to believe that our Universe was created without purpose. They are narrow-minded enough to discount the possibility of creation by God but, at the same time, believe in something as far-fetched as a chance origin 14 billion years ago. The previous pages contain only a few examples of how man's theories do not hold up to the Biblical account. There are many more grave problems that are revealed with thorough examination, some of which we will look at presently.

"Every word of God is pure"

The sun was created on day four as the greater light. It was to be for signs, seasons, days and years, as well as to give light upon the earth.

WHAT'S IN A DAY?

Based on the Biblical account, we have a clear seven day timeline of Creation.

Day One:
God created and divided light.

Day Two:
God created the firmament.

Day Three:
God created land and sea, and vegetation.

Day Four:
God created the heavenly lights.

Day Five:
God created sea creatures and fowl.

Day Six:
God created beasts, land creatures, and man.
He blessed what He had created.

Day Seven:
God rested from His work and hallowed the 7th day.

The Biblical account of the Creation week is written as a literal historical account and not an allegory or fable. The book of Genesis describes a 7 day Creation week, but were they really 24-hour days, or long spans of time as some teachers would have us believe?

Most scholars conclude that the Hebrew word 'YOM', or DAY, as found in the Creation account, refers to a literal, 24-hour day and not long periods of time as required by evolutionary theory. Careful study reveals that any time a numerical reference precedes the word 'yom', or day, it specifies a literal 24-hour day. This is what we see over and over again in Genesis 1.

Genesis 1:5:
"And God called the light Day, and the darkness he called Night. And the evening and the morning were the first day." In the original text, "Yom Echad"— "Day One".

If you had never researched these issues and read Genesis 1 for the first time, would you ever get the idea that when it says day, it means anything other than...day?

Another important consideration is the repetitive use of phrases like *"the evening and the morning were the first day"*. Not only are numbers associated with the word DAY, but the description *"evening and morning"* makes it plain that a literal 24-hour day is indicated.

Many people miss the importance of the seven-day Creation week. Scripture tell us: *In the beginning, God created the heaven and earth.* Not in billions of years, not in millions of years, not even in thousands of years, but in *six* literal *days*.

God *blessed the seventh day*, a literal 24 hours, *and hallowed it*, making it a Sabbath of rest, and the memorial of Creation. This is the original source of the seven-day week that we follow.

The Ten Commandments refer to a seven-day week, just as was designated in the beginning

> ***For in six days the LORD made heaven and earth, the sea, and all that in them is, and rested the seventh day: wherefore the LORD blessed the sabbath day, and hallowed it.***
>
> ***—Exodus 20:11***

Biblical days start and end at sundown. Evening represents the dark portion of the day after sundown, and morning represents the light portion from the time the sun comes up until that evening when it sets and starts another day.

Yeshua, Jesus Himself, spoke of the light and dark portions of a 24-hour day when He said, *"If any man walk in the day, he stumbleth not, because he seeth the light of this world. But if a man walk in the night, he stumbleth, because there is no light in him." —John 11:9-10*

Evolutionists truly stumble in the dark when they grasp at straws interpreting the plain language of the book of Genesis. Not only do they stumble, but their unproven theories cause others to do likewise. Just as our Savior stated: *"If the blind lead the blind, they shall both fall into the ditch." —Matthew 15:14*

ONE DAY = ONE THOUSAND YEARS?

One often used argument for non-literal days is the passage in second Peter which states: "*One day is with the Lord as a thousand years, and a thousand years as one day.*" Some attempt to equate each day of Creation with periods of time spanning one-thousand years. As we have seen in the Genesis account, there is no indication that *"day"* means anything other than a literal 24 hours.

In the book of Jonah we read that: "Jonah was in the belly of the fish three days and three nights." You would have a hard time finding someone who would argue that it was actually an extended stay of three-thousand years—yet when it comes to the statement: *"in six days the LORD made heaven and earth..."* some are more than willing to twist the plain truths of scripture.

If the plain language of the Creation account can be so easily re-interpreted, then what next? Will we continue to believe that Jesus was manifest in the flesh to die for our sins? Are the miracles that were performed by the disciples only allegorical accounts? Did Moses really live to be 120 years old? Was Jesus actually in the tomb three days and three nights?

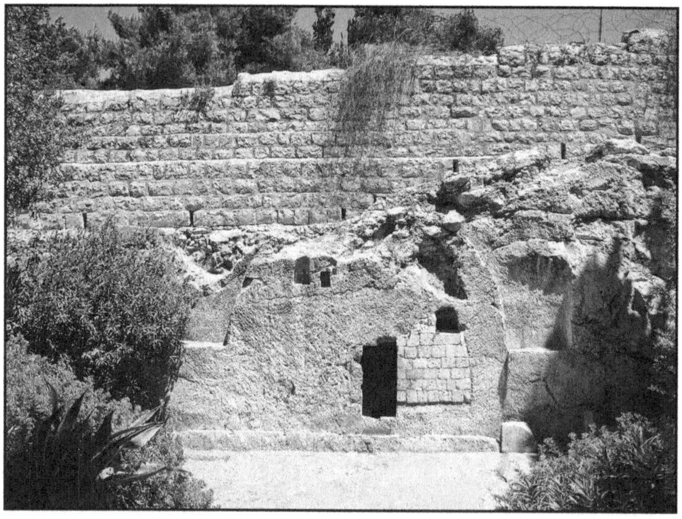

The Garden Tomb, Jerusalem, Israel

No matter how hard some attempt to deny the plain language of scripture as written by Moses, and confirmed by Jesus, the Creator Himself, the Bible tells us that it took only six evenings and mornings to create the Universe... Not nature running its course, but nothing less than a miracle, just as the birth of the Messiah, or the blind made to see.

THEISTIC EVOLUTION COMPROMISED CREATION

Today, there is an ever increasing demand for tolerance in churches. Many require Biblical views to be compromised in order that they might agree with theoretical science—compromise without regards to the cost.

Efforts to reinterpret Genesis in order to justify the Biblical account with evolutionary theory include: the theory of a local flood, Theistic Evolution, the Day-Age theory, the concept of Progressive Creation, the Gap theory, and other highly speculative ideas.

It is a mistake for Christians to concede to these speculative theories which oppose the plain words of Scripture. Those who are not yet believers will be confused when faced with a choice: Do we trust the Bible, or do we put our trust in theory?

Let's take a look at a few examples of what I call <u>compromised creation:</u>

THE DAY AGE THEORY:

The Day Age theory interprets each day of Creation to mean an age of time. These "ages" can be conveniently lengthened or shortened to fit any particular view. The Hebrew language of the Creation account specifies literal days composed of evenings and mornings.

THEISTIC EVOLUTION:

Theistic Evolution is the idea that what we see around us is the result of evolution, with one exception—the idea that God stepped in and guided when he was needed. The Bible states that at the end of day six *"God saw every thing that he had made, and, behold, it was very good."*

THE GAP THEORY:

The Gap theory puts a long gap of time between Genesis 1:1 and 1:2 calling for life and death long before the time of Adam. It is a theory that creates many more questions than it answers. The Bible tells us that Adam was the first man and that by man came death. Death came as a consequence of sin.

THE HEBREW WORDS TOHU AND BOHU:

תֹהוּ
TOHU
WITHOUT FORM
STRONGS 8414 DEFINITIONS INCLUDE:
EMPTY PLACE, WITHOUT FORM,
NOTHING, (THING OF) NOUGHT, VAIN
בֹהוּ
BOHU
VOID
STRONGS 922:
EMPTINESS, VOID

In regard to Genesis 1:2, it has been stated that the phrase *"the earth was without form and void"* refers to a destroyed Earth that was formed ages ago. The basis for this view rests on two words, "Tohu" and "Bohu," the two words translated as *"without form"* and *"void"*.

As we look at the original Hebrew however, we see that the word translated *"without form"* indicates an empty place, or nothing. The word translated *"void"* in Hebrew means just that: to be void, an emptiness.

THE LOCAL FLOOD THEORY:

The Local Flood theory calls for the dismissal of the global flood account as found in the Bible, even though a global flood is indicated by geology <u>all over the world.</u>

The Great Deluge as depicted by John Martin, 1834

> *"And the flood was forty days upon the earth; and the waters increased, and bare up the ark, and it was lift up above the earth... And the waters prevailed exceedingly upon the earth; and all the high hills, that were under the whole heaven, were covered. Fifteen cubits upward did the waters prevail; and the mountains were covered. And all flesh died that moved upon the earth, both of fowl, and of cattle, and of beast,*

> *and of every creeping thing that creepeth upon the earth, and every man: All in whose nostrils was the breath of life, of all that was in the dry land, died... Noah only remained alive, and they that were with him in the ark. And the waters prevailed upon the earth an hundred and fifty days."* —*Genesis 7:17-24*

Based on these theories of "Compromised Creation" that are being presented as fact, it is easy to understand how many people have come to believe in them. They have been made to look very appealing. Even so, when unproven theories disagree with the words of scripture, there is only one wise choice. Let's stop listening to man, pick up our Bibles, open them to Chapter 1, and read what it plainly says: "*In the beginning, God created the heaven and the earth."*

> *"For the invisible things of him from the creation of the world are clearly seen, being understood by the things that are made, even his eternal power and Godhead; so that they are without excuse: Because that, when they knew God, they glorified him not as God, neither were thankful; but became vain in their imaginations, and their foolish heart was darkened. Professing themselves to be wise, they became fools"* —*Romans 1:20-22*

As we have seen, theories of evolution lead us away from our Creator. They attempt to shift our focus from God and onto that which He created, as if the things that we see in the Universe and all around us have some innate ability to exist on their own. This is a very important consideration; for throughout the ages, mankind has had a great propensity to worship the created rather than the Creator Himself. Scripture informs us that those who do so do not like to retain God in their knowledge. Even though ***"the invisible things of him from the creation of the world are clearly seen"***—some have chosen to change the truth of God into a lie. We are told that ***Professing themselves to be wise, they became fools***...and that they are ***without excuse.***

CREATION AND THE GOSPEL OF CHRIST

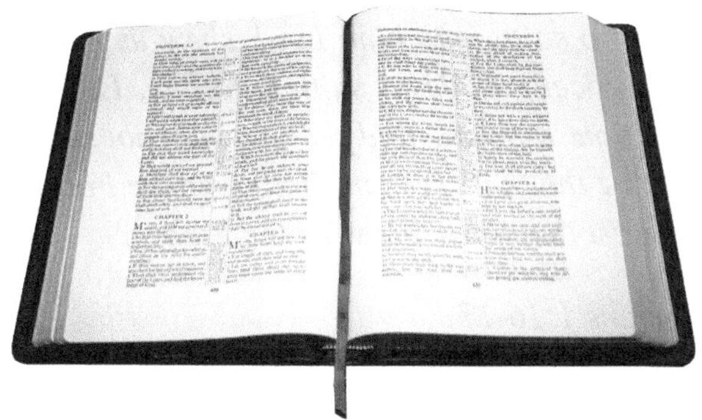

It is impossible to separate the Creation account as found in the book of Genesis from what we read in the New Testament—for it is all about our Creator:
Yeshua, Jesus Christ

John 1:1-3
In the beginning was the Word, and the Word was with God, and the Word was God. The same was in the

beginning with God. All things were made by him; and without him was not any thing made that was made.

John 1:10
He was in the world, and the world was made by him, and the world knew him not.

John 8:58
Jesus said unto them, Verily, verily, I say unto you, Before Abraham was, I am.

John 10:30
I and my Father are one.

John 14:7-9
If ye had known me, ye should have known my Father also: and from henceforth ye know him, and have seen him. Philip saith unto him, Lord, shew us the Father, and it sufficeth us. Jesus saith unto him, Have I been so long time with you, and yet hast thou not known me, Philip? he that hath seen me hath seen the Father; and how sayest thou then, Shew us the Father?

Colossians 1:16-17
For by him were all things created, that are in heaven, and that are in earth, visible and invisible, whether they be thrones, or dominions, or principalities, or powers: all things were created by him, and for him: And he is before all things, and by him all things consist.

1 Timothy 3:16
And without controversy great is the mystery of godliness: God was manifest in the flesh, justified in

the Spirit, seen of angels, preached unto the Gentiles, believed on in the world, received up into glory.

Revelation 1:8
I am Alpha and Omega, the beginning and the ending, saith the Lord, which is, and which was, and which is to come, the Almighty.

Isaiah 9:6
For unto us a child is born, unto us a son is given: and the government shall be upon his shoulder: and his name shall be called Wonderful, Counsellor, The mighty God, The everlasting Father, The Prince of Peace.

Isaiah 40:3
The voice of him that crieth in the wilderness, Prepare ye the way of the LORD, make straight in the desert a highway for our God.

Matthew 3:1-3 In those days came John the Baptist, preaching in the wilderness of Judaea, And saying, Repent ye: for the kingdom of heaven is at hand. For this is he that was spoken of by the prophet Esaias, saying, The voice of one crying in the wilderness, Prepare ye the way of the Lord, make his paths straight.

Colossians 2:8-9
Beware lest any man spoil you through philosophy and vain deceit, after the tradition of men, after the rudiments of the world, and not after Christ. For in him dwelleth all the fulness of the Godhead bodily.

Mankind is not the product of chance evolution. We are an important part of Creation that took place *"in the beginning"*. So important that: *"God so loved the world, that he gave his only begotten Son, that whosoever believeth in him should not perish, but have everlasting life."*

Just as the great wonders in the sky above are examples of His workmanship, we are His workmanship. On day six, we became the final creation in God's Universe—made *in His own image* and *after His own likeness—"Fearfully and wonderfully made."* Best of all, we are given the promise that as believers in Jesus, we have the incredible privilege of eternal life—an eternity to enjoy the unimaginable grandeur of His Universe.

> ***"As it is written, Eye hath not seen, nor ear heard, neither have entered into the heart of man, the things which God hath prepared for them that love him."***
>
> ***—1 Corinthians 2:9***

Chapter Four

No Kin To The Monkeys!

A LEAP OF FAITH

Human life is an amazing thing. Not only are we complex in design, but we have the ability and innate curiosity to ponder our own complexity. From this curiosity, some conclude that they are an anomaly of nature, the survival of the fittest in a chain of animal development. Others would conclude they have a special purpose, and marvel at the artistry of human design—the handiwork of the Creator.

The complexity of the human body baffles those who believe in chance origins. Candid scientists will admit they have no satisfactory NATURAL answer regarding the development of complex biological structures such as eyes and ears. Those who are evasive quickly point the finger at those who believe in God, saying that their religion has clouded their beliefs. The truth is just the opposite. It is the religion of evolutionary science that has clouded the minds of its advocates. It takes a giant leap of faith to trust that everything is the end result of nothing—From shambles to structure over 14 billion years.

WHAT DID THE CREATOR SAY?

Recently an article appeared on CNN entitled "Jesus would believe in evolution and so should you." Perhaps the author failed to read the words of Jesus when He said: *"From the beginning of the creation God made them male and female."*

The article states as fact: "We now know that the human race began millions of years ago in Africa - not thousands of years ago in the Middle East, as the story in Genesis suggests."

The author presents his statements as fact; yet, he does not even know that the Biblical account never specifies where life began. Where was the Garden of Eden located? No one knows for sure. The writer is so enamoured with evolutionary "science" and the twisted facts behind it, that he doesn't even know what the Bible actually says.

The blasphemous CNN article states: "There is much evidence for evolution. The most compelling comes from the study of genes."

DNA molecules provide the genetic instructions necessary for the development and function of all living organisms. A cursory examination of DNA reveals that it is incredibly complex. It would be impossible to create the DNA found in most life forms though chance, even given the evolutionary time frame of millions of years.

According to the Gallup Poll which the CNN article cites, more people still believe that God created humans a relatively short time ago (What we read in the Bible), than do people that believe God used evolution to form us from nothing. Yes, most people still believe that God created the heaven and the Earth in six days—including mankind as a complete being.

"The wisdom of this world is foolishness with God... The Lord knoweth the thoughts of the wise, that they are vain."
—1 Corinthians 3:19

CHARLES DARWIN - A STEP TOO FAR:

Charles Darwin was born in Shrewsbury, England. At the age of 19, he entered the University of Cambridge, where he studied to become a Clergyman in the Anglican Church. Darwin later wrote that his time at Cambridge was sadly wasted, and that he was much more interested in collecting beetles than anything he had studied at Cambridge.

After finishing his studies, Darwin was invited to accompany Captain Robert FitzRoy on a survey expedition to South America aboard the HMS Beagle.

HMS Beagle - 1820-1845
Darwin's journals of the Beagle's second expedition were published under the title "The Voyage of the Beagle"

During his voyage, Darwin noticed differences in the beaks of finches and various birds that allowed them to adapt to their surroundings.

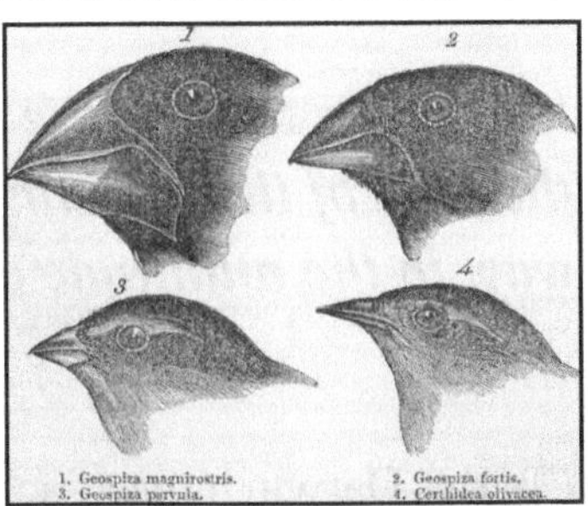

He pioneered the well-known concept of micro-evolution based on his observations. Life, when placed in different environmental situations, has an amazing ability to adapt to its surroundings.

THAT is observable science.... However, Darwin took it one step further and began to theorize that perhaps all life originated ages ago from a single organism. He guessed that if animals could indeed adapt in such a way, then if you gave them enough time, perhaps an animal could become a human...

A macro-evolutionary tale that was just wild enough to catch people's attention—and those who weren't grounded in the Bible fell for it. According to the Bible, that is simply not true.

No, an amoeba will not turn into a frog, or a whale, or a man, no matter how many millions of years you give it.

"It is time to seek the LORD... Ye have eaten the fruit of lies: because thou didst trust in thy way, in the multitude of thy mighty men."
—Hosea 10:12-13

Charles Darwin himself acknowledged a Creator in the closing comments of the later editions of his book On the Origin of Species. He says: "There is grandeur in this view of life, with its several powers, having been originally breathed by the Creator into a few forms or into one." We discover, however, in the very first edition, the absence of the words "by the Creator". Later in life, he admitted: "I have long regretted that I truckled to public opinion & used a Pentateuchal term of creation, by which I really meant 'appeared' by some wholly unknown process"

THIS is the two-faced man that scientists look up to as revolutionary in his field.

MONKEY BUSINESS

Since the time Darwin's book was written, modern day evolutionary thought has developed to the point that many respected scientists believe that they themselves are nothing more than sophisticated apes.

You don't need a PhD to realize that there is something very wrong with the concept of macro-evolution. Over 150 years after Darwin's publication, we are still only skimming the surface when it comes to understanding the complexity of human life. Mathematics reveals the improbability of chance human origins and point overwhelmingly to a designer.

Despite man's attempts to reduce us to prehistoric primates, you and I aren't animals. We are fearfully and wonderfully made.

"God saw every thing that he had made, and, behold, it was very good." —Genesis 1:31

CHARLES LYELL
1797-1875
British Geologist and Author of "Principles of Geology"

Charles Darwin was greatly influenced by a man named Charles Lyell, who along with James Hutton, advanced the idea of uniformitarianism and the dating of fossils by way of what has become known as the Geologic Column.

In a letter to an English Geologist by the name of George Scrope, Lyell plainly states that his studies, published in the periodical Quarterly Review would "free the science from Moses".

He said that the Christianity of his day had seen "the mischief and scandal brought on them by the Mosaic System" and that "If we don't irritate...we shall carry them with us". There is little doubt that today, just as Lyell predicted, many Christians have been carried right along with the evolutionists who reject the writings of Moses. By careful wording, subtle tactics, and a gradual introduction into the school system, they have avoided the "irritation" that would have made most Christians immediately spot the falsity. Now, evolution has become the "scientific" norm and is taught by many to be compatible with the scriptures.

Has Lyell's work "freed the science"? Regrettably, it has made science blind to any of the history contained in the Bible. This history could answer many of their greatest and most difficult questions.

THE GEOLOGIC COLUMN

Charles Lyell's Geologic Column, with its colorful graphs, is displayed in nature museums around the world. The concept of an orderly Geologic Column is taught as if it were well-documented. Even so, the Geologic Column is largely a figment of Lyell's imagination. It is rarely found in nature. The column is supposedly a multi-layered index of geology dated by the fossils found in each layer.

In other words, if you find trilobites in a certain strata, it must be from a designated age of time dating back millions of years ago.

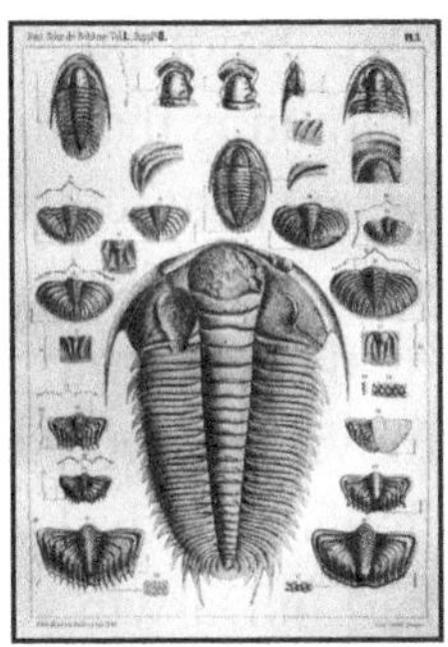

Right: Trilobites - extinct marine arthropods

Below: The proposed geologic timeline as outlined in Lyell's "Geologic Column" - a model still in use despite very little correlation with factual evidence

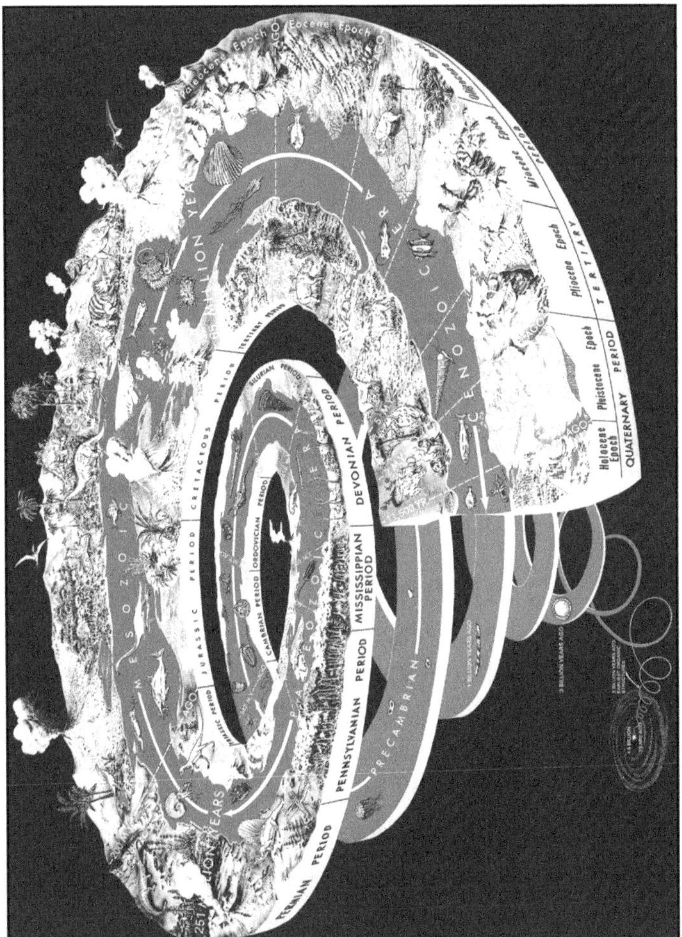

One major problem with the concept of a geological column is that the fossils are seldom seen in a precise order. That, coupled with very little scientific basis, is today surprisingly regarded as good science. Elements of the geologic column have become the subject of movies in popular culture, school textbooks, and entire fields of study. Lyell's work also played an instrumental part in Darwin's formation of evolutionary theory.

Lyell scoffed at the idea that *"In the beginning God created,"* and it was Lyell that dated the layers and fossils based primarily on a vivid imagination, long before the time of most current dating procedures.

"There shall come in the last days scoffers, walking after their own lusts, And saying, Where is the promise of his coming? for since the fathers fell asleep, all things continue as they were from the beginning of the creation... The heavens and the earth, which are now, by the same word are kept in store, reserved unto fire against the day of judgment and perdition of ungodly men." —2 Peter 3:3-7

UNIFORMITARIANISM

Charles Lyell also played an instrumental part in the idea of an old Earth and slow geologic change. These elements eventually became major components of evolutionary theory. Uniformitarianism is the idea that "the present is the key to the past" and that through a slow and methodical process, natural laws have always worked in the same way. In contrast, the Bible states that the heaven and Earth were created in six days.

ERNST HAECKEL

Dr. Ernst Haeckel was an early convert to Darwinism, and his depiction of the progressive states of vertebrate development became widely used in scientific literature. Charles Darwin used copies of these illustrations in his own books, calling them "works of undoubted accuracy".

You will notice in Haeckel's illustrations, in the first stages of all embryonic development are indications of gill slits—even in humans! The theory known as Biogenetic Law is the idea that the embryos of all complex animals go through the same stages of development as those of their evolutionary ancestors.

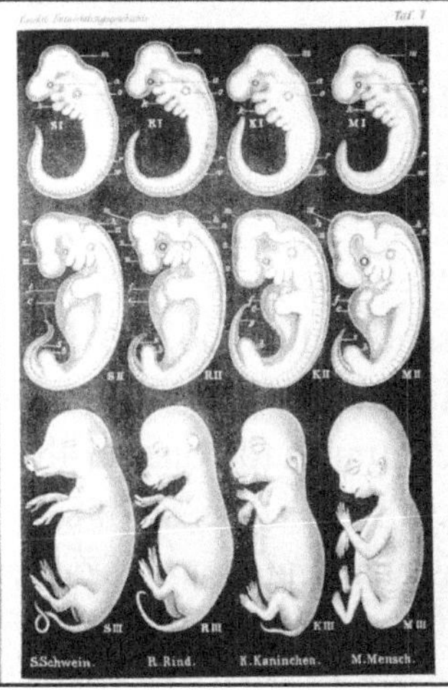

Above: An illustration of the "gill slits" in the embryonic development of diverse creatures. Proven to be false, yet still circulated today.

WILHELM HIS

In 1874, a Swiss professor by the name of Wilhelm His documented the fact that Haeckel had altered his drawings to show gill slits in an effort to support the theory of evolution.

That did not slow the majority of evolutionists down at all. They continued to advance the theory of Biogenetic Law. Finally, in 1956, it was stated in the Everyman's introduction of Darwin's Origin of the Species, 6th edition, that Haeckel had altered his drawings and that biogenetic law as proof of evolution was valueless. Even the popular evolutionist, the late Stephen Jay Gould, admitted that Haeckel had "exaggerated the similarities by idealizations and omissions".

It seems that Haeckel's science was somewhat green around the gills.

Well over 130 years after the time of Haeckel's work, school textbooks still use drawings based on his falsified illustrations. Today's evolutionary agenda continues to conquer the vulnerable minds of children with a false sense of science, while the Biblical record is challenged and even forbidden in our classrooms.

The Christian religion, being replaced as the religion of evolution, is warmly embraced.

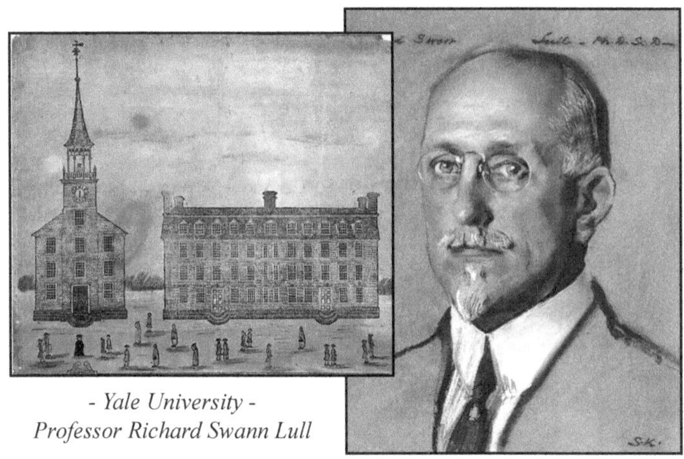

- Yale University -
Professor Richard Swann Lull

AN APE OF A HOAX

Yale University was established in 1701 to train Christian ministers. Today, its department of religious studies offers a wide array of courses that cover the major religions of the world. By the 1920's, the teaching of evolution was the focus of the famous Yale Peabody Museum, recognized as the first natural history museum to depict human origins in terms of organic evolution. Its director Richard Swann Lull invited the public to explore what has been described as the overt depiction of human evolution by way of exhibits designed to attract the interest of children.

In 1929, Professor Lull published a book entitled Organic Evolution. He believed that man was just one more kind of animal—a Primate, the title indicating headship of the animal kingdom. He believed that apes are our next of kin and that the reason we are not hairy all over is because we started wearing clothes:

> "Still another specialization is the loss of hair from the body, possibly as a result of the acquisition of artificial clothing. The evidence for this belief cited by Matthew (1915) follows: "(I) It is accompanied by an exceptional and progressive delicacy of skin, quite unsuited to travel in tropical forests. I do not know of any thin-haired or hairless tropical animal whose skin is not more or less thickened for protection against chafing, the attacks of insects, etc. (2) The loss [of hair] is most complete on the back and abdomen. The arms and the legs and, in the male, the chest, retain hair much more persistently. This is just what would naturally happen if the loss of hair were due to the wearing of clothes, — at first and for a long time, a skin thrown over the shoulders and tied around the waist. But if the loss of hair were conditioned by climate it should, as it invariably does among animals, disappear first on the under side of the body and the limbs and be retained longest on the back and shoulders."
>
> —Organic Evolution, 1929; Lull

In his book, Dr. Lull presented the skeletal remains of a supposed ape-like human known as Piltdown man as evidence for evolution. Supposedly, a missing link had been discovered. It was later determined by respected paleontologists that Piltdown man was nothing more than a human cranium matched up with an orangutan jaw with the teeth filed down to look like those of humans—a total fraud.

John Cooke's 1915 painting of the Piltdown scientists
A portrait of Charles Darwin hangs on the wall in the background

Over 40 years passed from the time the supposed fragments of Piltdown Man were discovered until their exposure as a hoax. Perhaps it's time to take a closer look at some of the other supposed "evidence" for evolution.

LUCY THE CHIMP

The world-famous "Lucy" hominid is another supposed scientific link between human beings and apes. She was found under extremely unusual circumstances in Ethiopia, in the fall of 1974.

Anthropologist Donald Johanson and Tom Gray, his student, were exploring alone in a gully that had previously been searched by other workers to no avail.

Paleoanthropologist Donald Johanson

Surprisingly, they happened upon a limited number of bones and skeletal remains. Picking up bone fragments all over the gully, they were amazed to discover they had found approximately 40 percent of an ape-like creature. Parts and pieces including arm fragments, a femur, a pelvis, and some ribs, were then patched together into what appeared to be a common chimpanzee with one exception: The hips and legs found indicated that this ape walked on two feet, not four.

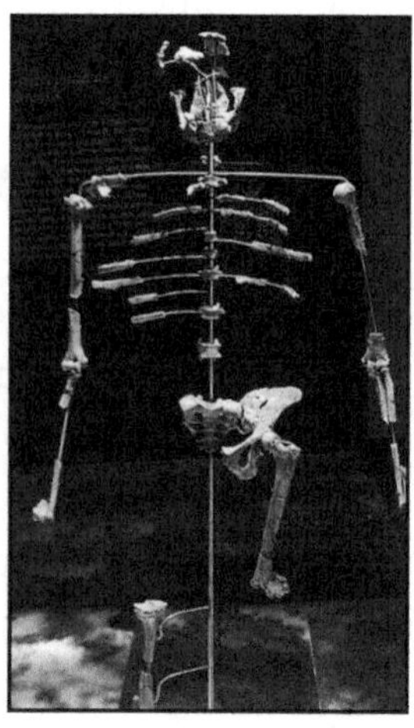

Lucy, the proposed "prehistoric ancestor to humans" revealed interesting characteristics: She probably weighed a little over 60 pounds, and was only around three-and-a-half feet tall—quite small for a human-like ancestor. The size and shape of the skull fragments indicated a very small brain, similar to..... an ape.

According to highly speculative radio-metric dating methods, Lucy was thought to have been around 3.2 million years old. How did they arrive at her age? By testing some ash found around her fragmented remains.

Perhaps Lucy isn't the only one with a small brain...

WHAT IS MAN

Most people have been taught that we as humans are nothing more than a product of evolution—that millions of years ago, you and I were only tiny organisms swimming in a pond. Some would lead us to believe that over time, we began to hang by our tails from trees and eat ants out of the ground—that somehow, we evolved into the human species and became smarter than other primates.

While we *have* advanced technologically and knowledge has truly increased, it seems that we as humans have done everything *but* get smarter. Wars still rage on today just as they did thousands of years ago. Lawlessness abounds and, in some cases, is even rewarded in today's society. Just as in the past, men still believe that they can be their own gods.

Even some professing Christ would tell us that we can believe in evolution and the Biblical record at the same time. If, however, we place our trust in the Bible as the literal Word of God, we know that this is not possible. *"As for God, his way is perfect; the word of the LORD is tried: he is a buckler to all them that trust in him."*

—2 Samuel 22:31

Who can be so bold to say that there is nothing special about the human race? When we stop to consider the intricate mechanisms of the human body, it is nothing less than incredible.

"I am fearfully and wonderfully made: marvellous are thy works..."
—Psalms 139:14

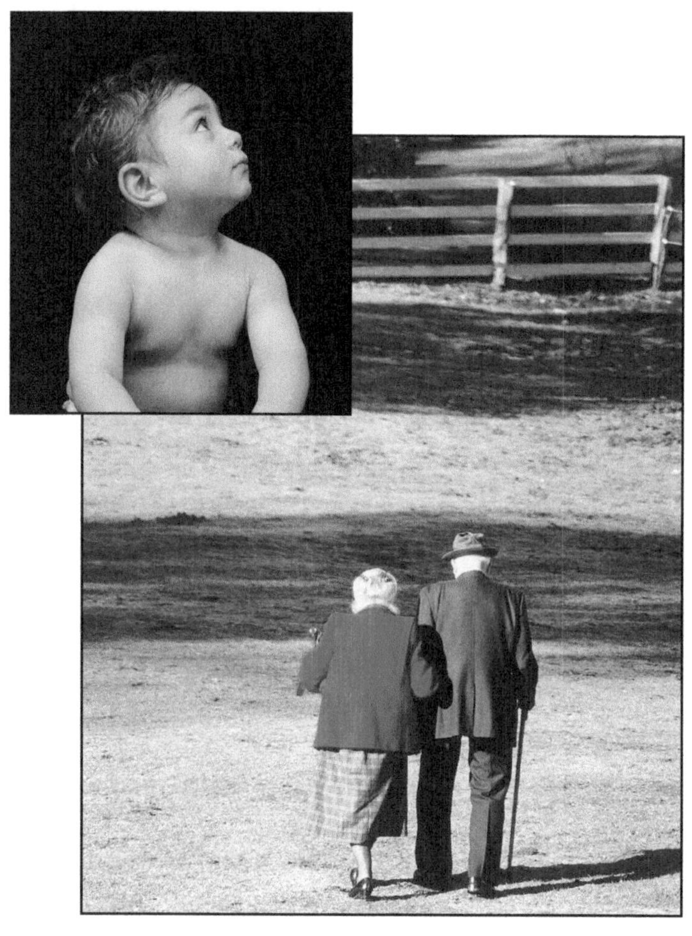

CHAPTER FIVE
A SPECIAL EARTH

THE GALACTIC HABITABLE ZONE

When we look at the Universe in all its vastness, it is easy to think of the Earth as small and insignificant. But Earth has some extraordinary characteristics that enable it to survive in a Universe that is, for the most part, hostile to life.

The Earth occupies a precise safe zone known as the Galactic Habitable Zone. Our location within this zone is no coincidence. The book of Isaiah informs us: *"God himself that formed the earth ...he formed it to be inhabited."*

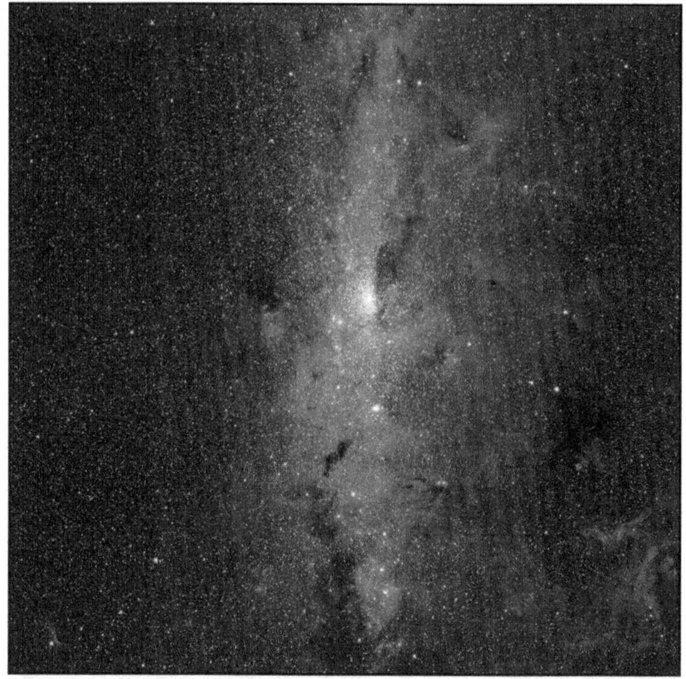

Our Milky Way Galaxy in infrared light. Many believe that the area in the center of this photograph contains a black hole.

OUR GALAXY

When we look into the night sky and see a bright 'band' of stars stretching from one end of the heavens to the other, we are observing our galaxy, the Milky Way. The term galaxy comes from the Greek word 'gala' which means milk. The Milky Way is a spiral galaxy consisting of an estimated 200 to 400 billion stars. Our sun is one of those stars.

Many scientists believe that the center of our galaxy is composed of a massive black hole. If that is true, any object situated near that area would be in danger of being pulled in and disappearing forever. If the Earth was situated in an area near the Milky Way's center, it would be unlikely to survive for even a short period of time. On the other hand, the outer edges of the galaxy would pose a threat to our existence as well. In these regions, the heavier elements essential for life are thought to be very rare—perhaps even non-existent.

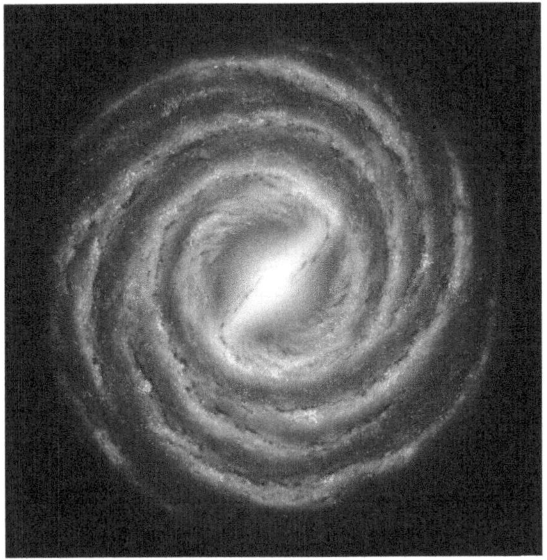

- Milky Way Galaxy -
Artist Conception of the spiral structure

It is interesting to note that our location, presumed to be between the Sagittarius and Perseus arms of the Milky Way, enables Earth to safely exist without the threat of powerful supernovae, black holes, stellar collisions, or elemental deficiencies. In short, we just happen to be in the best possible position in our galaxy for life to exist.

CIRCUM-STELLAR HABITABLE ZONE

Every star we see in the night sky is a burning mass of plasma similar to the sun. Even so, our sun is not just any star. Ninety-five percent of all stars are less massive. Smaller stars are found in abundance, and the size of our sun is a very important consideration.

If the Sun were smaller, then the habitable zone for Earth would be much further inward, and that could induce synchronous rotation. In this case, the gravity from a small Sun would cause one side of the Earth to continually face the Sun. In other words, there would be no day and night, only boiling temperatures on one side and freezing temperatures on the other.

Our planet Earth is about 93 million miles from the Sun and is situated in a very narrow band that supports habitability. If the Earth was only 5 percent closer to the Sun, it would become like the planet Venus, *boiling hot*, and uninhabitable. However, if we were just 20 percent farther away, our planet would resemble Mars, *freezing...* and still uninhabitable.

If Earth were on a very elliptical orbit around the Sun, then it would be alternately too close and too far away for life to be sustained. Instead, we find that Earth has a nearly circular orbit, perfect for life.

EARTH'S GEO-MAGNETIC FIELD

The Earth was specially designed to protect us from harmful cosmic radiation.

Our planet is thought to have a liquid iron core. Why is this significant? Earth's Geo-Magnetic fields are believed to be produced by this liquid iron core.

The Geo-Magnetic field that surrounds the Earth enables our compasses to be used as a means of navigation, but more importantly, it acts as a deflection shield to protect us from solar wind and cosmic radiation. Without this field, our planet would become as Mercury. It would constantly be swept with the solar wind making Earth barren, desolate, and void of life.

There ARE times when some of the charged particles from the solar wind enter the Earth's upper atmosphere. These are observed through a colorful display known as the Aurora Borealis and Australis, or more commonly, the Northern and Southern Lights.

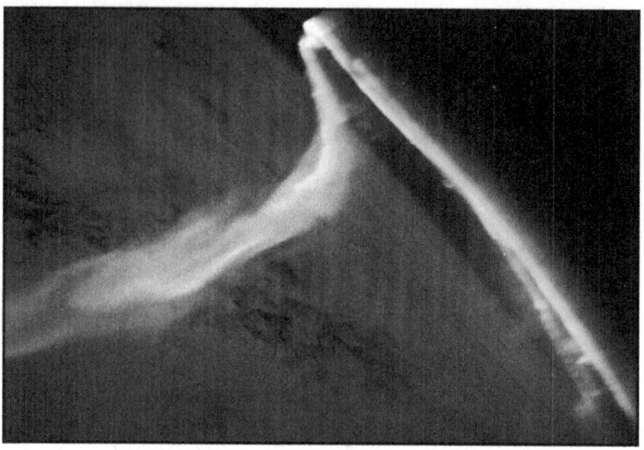

Aurora - As seen from space

Earth's Geo-Magnetic fields are one more example of our Creator's incredible design.

AN EXCEPTIONAL PLANET

While many scientists today claim that the Earth was formed by chance from cosmic dust, billions of years ago, a close examination of our planet reveals that it was carefully designed.

SHIELDING PLANETS

Earth's position in the solar system is such that the large outer planets, known as "gas giants," circle and protect us as they revolve farther out in space. Dangerous cosmic debris is pulled in by the massive gravity of the outer planets instead of proceeding closer to Earth.

- Comet Shoemaker-Levy -
Above: Comet breaking apart as it approaches Jupiter
Left: Dark spots on Jupiter immediately after impact

A perfect example of this was in 1994 when comet Shoemaker-Levy broke apart into 21 pieces, as the tremendous gravity of Jupiter pulled those fragments in.

The comet was traveling around 133,000 MPH as it approached. At that speed, you and I could travel from New York to L.A. in less than a minute and a half. The fragments collided with the strength of 1 million hydrogen bombs and sent a mushroom shaped cloud of gas 1,000 miles high.

As we see, the large outer planets do indeed attract debris with their strong gravitational fields.

DRY LAND

A terrestrial planet is also necessary for human life to exist. Many planets are composed entirely of gas.

EARTH'S ATMOSPHERE

Our atmosphere is also unique when compared to other planets. Surrounding our planet, gravity maintains a layer of gases essential to life. This layer regulates the temperatures through the absorption of solar radiation. Only the Earth's atmosphere is transparent. In addition, only Earth has the correct combination of gases for life to exist. These conditions have not been found anywhere else in the Universe.

Nitrogen............. 78.09%
Oxygen............... 20.95%
Argon................... 0.93%
Carbon Dioxide.... 0.039%

Another consideration is atmospheric pressure. Earth has an atmospheric pressure of approximately 14.7 pounds per square inch at sea level. In comparison, the atmospheric pressure of Venus would be a crushing 90 times that of Earth.

LIQUID WATER

Another consideration is the fact that we have liquid water which is essential for life. Not only is it necessary for human survival, but it helps transport nutrients through the Earth and absorbs heat from the sun to regulate temperatures.

GRAVITY

The size and mass of our planet is perfect for moderated gravity. As an example, a 150 pound person here on Earth would weigh approximately 350 pounds on Jupiter.

DESIGNED WITH PURPOSE

We have discussed many unique factors. If only one were slightly off, life would not be possible. Our special Earth was carefully designed with a purpose by a loving Creator.

> ***"...Thus saith the LORD that created the heavens; God himself that formed the earth and made it; he hath established it, he created it not in vain, he formed it to be inhabited." —Isaiah 45:18***

Chapter Six
The Moon

THE ORIGIN OF THE MOON

Genesis 1:16 tells us that the Moon was created by God on day four, as a light to rule the night. Over the years, astronomers have attempted to take God out of the picture, by way of various theories as to how the Moon could have originated through cosmic evolution: the Fission theory, the Capture theory, the Nebular theory, and one of the more recent, the Collision theory.

The following is a direct quote from the Astrophysics Science Division at NASA / GSFC:

> ***The Fission Theory*** *"proposes that the Moon was once part of the Earth and somehow separated from the Earth early in the history of the solar system. The present Pacific Ocean basin is the most popular site for the part of the Earth from which the Moon came. This theory was thought possible since the Moon's composition resembles that of the Earth's mantle and a rapidly spinning Earth could have cast off the Moon from its outer layers. However, the present-day Earth-Moon system should contain "fossil evidence" of this rapid spin and it does not. Also, this hypothesis does not have a natural explanation for the extra baking the lunar material has received."*

> ***The Capture Theory*** *"proposes that the Moon was formed somewhere else in the solar system, and was later captured by the gravitational field of the Earth. The Moon's different chemical composition could be explained if it formed elsewhere in the solar system, however, capture into the Moon's present orbit is very improbable. Something would have to slow it down by just the right amount at just the right time, and scientists are reluctant to believe in such "fine tuning". Also, this hypothesis does not have a natural explanation for the extra baking the lunar material has received."*

The Condensation Theory *"proposes that the Moon and the Earth condensed individually from the nebula that formed the solar system, with the Moon formed in orbit around the Earth. However, if the Moon formed in the vicinity of the Earth it should have nearly the same composition. Specifically, it should possess a significant iron core, and it does not. Also, this hypothesis does not have a natural explanation for the extra baking the lunar material has received."*

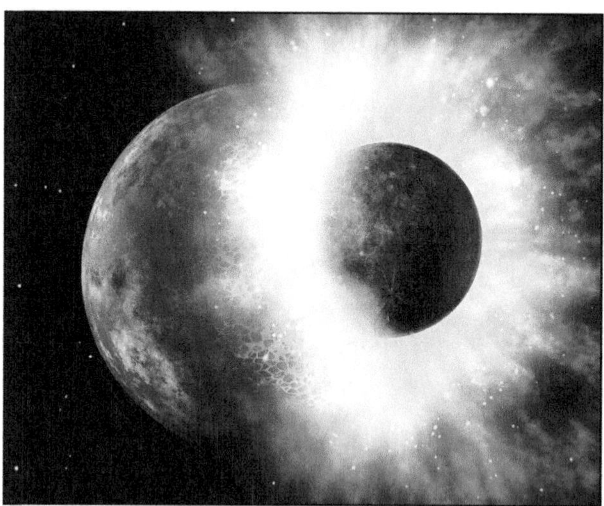

The Giant Impactor Theory *(sometimes called The Ejected Ring Theory) "proposes that a planetesimal (or small planet) the size of Mars struck the Earth just after the formation of the solar system, ejecting large volumes of heated material from the outer layers of both objects. A disk of orbiting material was formed, and this matter eventually stuck together to form the Moon in orbit around the Earth. This theory can explain*

why the Moon is made mostly of rock and how the rock was excessively heated. Furthermore, we see evidence in many places in the solar system that such collisions were common late in the formative stages of the solar system...

"In the mid-1970s, scientists proposed the giant impact scenario for the formation of the Moon. The idea was that an off-center impact of a roughly Mars-sized body with a young Earth could provide Earth with its fast initial spin, and eject enough debris into orbit to form the Moon. If the ejected material came primarily from the mantles of the Earth and the impactor, the lack of a sizeable lunar core was easily understood, and the energy of the impact could account for the extra heating of lunar material required by analysis of lunar rock samples obtained by the Apollo astronauts.

"For nearly a decade, the giant impact theory was not believed by most scientists. However, in 1984, a conference devoted to lunar origin prompted a critical comparison of the existing theories. The giant impact theory emerged from this conference with nearly consensus support by scientists, enhanced by new models of planet formation that suggested large impacts were actually quite common events in the late stages of terrestrial planet formation.

"The basic idea is this: about 4.45 billion years ago, a young planet Earth -- a mere 50 million years old at the time and not the solid object we know today-- experienced the largest impact event of its history. Another planetary body with roughly the mass of Mars had formed nearby with an orbit that placed it on a collision course with Earth. When young Earth and this rogue body collided, the energy involved was 100 million times larger than the much later event believed to have wiped out the dinosaurs. The early giant collision destroyed the rogue body, likely vaporized the upper layers of Earth's mantle, and ejected large amounts of debris into Earth orbit. Our Moon formed from this debris."
—Astrophysics Science Division at NASA / GSFC

As we have seen, the Collision theory proposes the formation of the Moon about 4.5 billion years ago, not on day 4 of Creation as the book of Genesis states. There is an extremely important decision that must be made: Are we going to believe what the Bible says, or are we going to believe in the ever-changing theories of man? Those who choose the theories of man must make another vital decision: If the plain language of the Creation account can be so easily discounted, then what other portions of scripture will one willingly deny?

"Stablish thy word unto thy servant, who is devoted to thy fear." —Psalm 119:38

ROCHE LIMIT

Édouard Roche, (1820-1883), was a French astronomer who studied the effects of gravity on moons. He discovered that mathematically, if a large object came too close to a planet, it would be broken into pieces.

Based on the proposed Roche Limit, some scientists believe that the theorized 'Mars-sized object' of the Collision theory could not have reached the Earth without being shattered into pieces.

Despite the attempts of secular scientists to explain the origin of the Moon, over time, each theory has been replaced with a new evolutionary theory. One day, perhaps they will learn that the Bible was correct after all. The Moon was formed <u>intact</u> on the fourth day of Creation.

OUR AMAZING MOON

In the book of Genesis, we're told that God created the Moon to be for light in the firmament of the heaven. It was also to be for signs, seasons, days, and years. Our Moon is the most visually stunning celestial object in the night because it is so easy to see, even without the use of a telescope or binoculars. While we can study the smaller characteristics of the Moon with high-powered optics, many of its main surface features can be seen with the unaided eye.

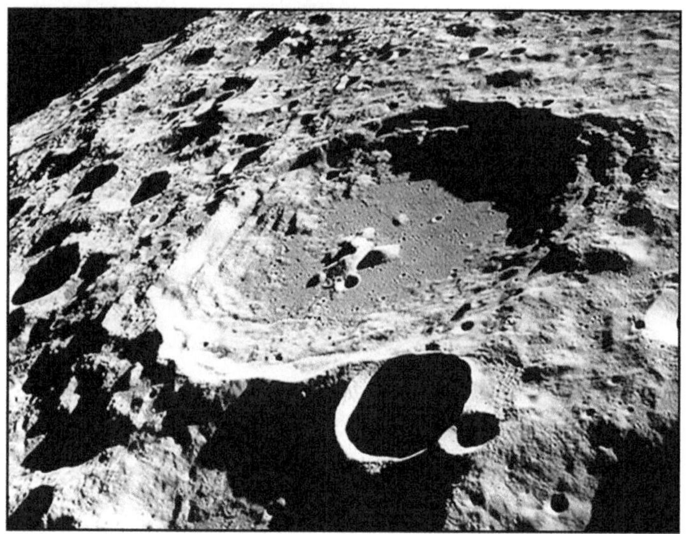

MOON FACTS:

- The Moon is, on average, 239,000 miles from Earth; it's just over a quarter the size of the Earth. Compared to its host planet, it is the largest proportionally of all the other moons in the Solar System.

- Because of its size, ocean tides here on Earth are created by the gravity of the Moon, which helps to circulate the warm and cold waters of the ocean.

- Unlit areas of the Moon's surface can reach a shuddering temperature of minus 280 degrees Fahrenheit, while the "sun-lit" daytime portions reach temperatures of up to 260 degrees.

- Our Moon occupies an elliptical or oval shaped orbit around the Earth and completes one orbit every 27 and one-third days. It spins on its axis once each orbit, meaning that we always see the same side.

- An occurrence known as “libration” results in the Moon rocking back and forth, and it allows us to see more than just one side. Because of libration, we can see 59 percent of the Moon’s surface.

- Unlike the Sun, the Moon does not generate its own light, but, rather, its surface reflects the light of the Sun. Because of this, we can calculate and observe what is known as a lunar eclipse.

- Lunar eclipses occur as the Earth passes between the Sun and Moon and can take place up to three times per year. They also give us great insight into scientific principles and offer us the rare opportunity to see the shadow of the spherical Earth.

There is no doubt that the Moon is a unique object designed by our Creator with its own special purpose. One day in the future, the book of Isaiah tells us that the lights in the heavens will no longer be needed:

“The sun shall be no more thy light by day; neither for brightness shall the moon give light unto thee: but the LORD shall be unto thee an everlasting light, and thy God thy glory.” —Isaiah 60:19

- Crew of the Apollo 8 Moon Mission, 1968 -
The first manned mission to orbit the Moon

FLY ME TO THE MOON

Today, our government wants to take God out of its decisions, prayer out of the schools, and the Ten Commandments out of the courtroom. Today, many American astronomers embrace evolutionary theory as scientific fact. Even so, our nation's scientists have not always been opposed to the words of scripture.

Not so long ago in 1968, the Apollo 8 mission was launched, becoming the first manned mission to orbit the Moon. The following monumental speech was given by the astronauts as they orbited the Moon—the Creation account directly from the book of Genesis:

William Anders:

"We are now approaching lunar sunrise and, for all the people back on Earth, the crew of Apollo 8 has a message that we would like to send to you:

In the beginning God created the heaven and the earth. And the earth was without form, and void; and darkness was upon the face of the deep. And the Spirit of God moved upon the face of the waters. And God said, Let there be light: and there was light. And God saw the light, that it was good: and God divided the light from the darkness."

Jim Lovell:

"And God called the light Day, and the darkness he called Night. And the evening and the morning were the first day. And God said, Let there be a firmament in the midst of the waters, and let it divide the waters from the waters. And God made the firmament, and divided the waters which were under the firmament from the waters which were above the firmament: and it was so. And God called the firmament Heaven. And the evening and the morning were the second day."

Frank Borman:
"And God said, Let the waters under the heavens be gathered together unto one place, and let the dry land appear: and it was so. And God called the dry land Earth; and the gathering together of the waters called he Seas: and God saw that it was good.

And from the crew of Apollo 8, we close with good night, good luck, a Merry Christmas, and God bless all of you - all of you on the good Earth."

Since that time, many have questioned the very existence of God. According to the New Testament, Jesus Christ was the Creator. Those of us who believe on Him must stand strong in the faith and continue to preach the truth of the Bible, proclaiming the Gospel to all nations.

In the beginning, God created the heaven and the Earth in six days. And behold, it was very good.

WALKING ON THE MOON

Neil Armstrong - First on Moon

In 1969, during the Apollo 11 space mission, astronaut Neil Armstrong was the first man to set foot on the surface of the Moon. The Lunar Module landed in an area known as "Mare Tranquillitatis" or the "Sea of Tranquility". This site was chosen because it was one of the flattest and smoothest places where they could land safely and collect samples—a tranquil place. During this mission, the astronauts set up a retro-reflector on the lunar surface. That experiment has enabled scientists to shoot a laser beam at the reflector. Based on this technology, the Moon's distance is said to be receding from Earth at a rate of 1 to 2 inches per year. The Apollo 14 and 15 missions have contributed to this operation by installing additional reflectors.

As a result of the collection of data made possible by the retroreflectors, scientists now calculate that the Moon is receding at a rate of approximately 1.5 inches per year. Based on mathematical calculations, the Moon would have been in contact with the surface of the Earth long before its proposed age of 4.6 billion years—a serious problem for evolutionary astrophysicists.

The last three Apollo missions employed the Lunar Roving Vehicle, or Moon Buggy. Apollo 15, the first to use the Moon Buggy, landed at the northern end of the Apennine Mountain Range, near Mount Hadley, and spent a good deal of time exploring in the Rover. Over the course of the six lunar Apollo missions, 842 pounds of lunar material was brought back for analysis. The lunar space missions came to an end with Apollo 17, which, on December 7, 1972, became the first night launch.

Dr. Wernher von Braun (1912-1977) was instrumental in the NASA space program, and the Director of the Marshall Space Flight Center. Since the time of the space race, NASA lost one of its greatest scientists, with the passing of Dr. von Braun.

As a scientist, Dr. Wernher von Braun strongly believed that Creation was far too complex to have been formed by chance. He made the following powerful statement in reference to his belief in Jesus Christ: "We should not be dismayed by the relative insignificance of our own planet in the vast universe as modern science now sees it. In fact God deliberately reduced Himself to the stature of humanity in order to visit the earth in person... The stage was set for a situation without parallel in the history of the earth. God would visit creatures and they would nail Him to the cross!" (Hill, 1976)

Today, while evolutionary theory has become the scientific norm, Von Braun stated: "One cannot be exposed to the law and order of the universe without concluding that there must be design and purpose behind it all." (See Appendix Two—Von Braun)

THE SUN AND MOON NO MORE

Throughout this chapter we have seen how our existence on Earth is based not on random chance but is reliant upon innumerous finely tuned factors, all working in unison.

Our position in the Universe, the Milky Way galaxy, and the Solar System, is essential for Human survival. Our Moon, a single, large satellite, is exclusive to Earth, providing for the regulation of tides, and the stability of our axis. We have liquid water and a unique atmosphere.

All these factors and yet only minute changes in just one would upset the balance, making life impossible. What an amazing place indeed, and according to Genesis, it was created fully functioning in only six days. The Earth, filled with its wonder and complex design, does not even compare to what we can expect in the future:

> ***"The sun shall be no more thy light by day; neither for brightness shall the moon give light unto thee: but the LORD shall be unto thee an everlasting light, and thy God thy glory." —Isaiah 60:19***

CHAPTER SEVEN
THE STARS OF HEAVEN

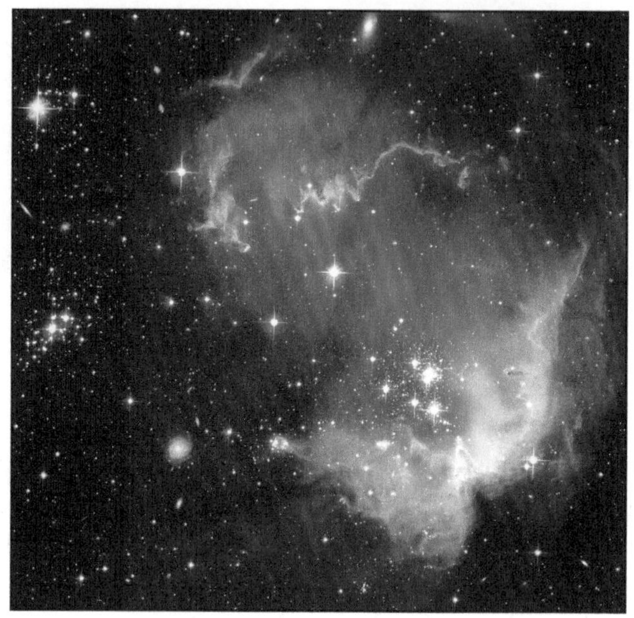

DISTANCE TO THE STARS

We know that distant stars and galaxies are incredibly far away. Scientists have attempted to measure the distances of these celestial objects using various methods. One of the most popular methods is known as Stellar Parallax, the use of trigonometry to determine distance.

Stellar Parallax is the apparent shift of a close star in relation to distant stars that is caused by a change in the position of the observer.

The stars are not actually moving; they just seem like they are because the person looking at them has moved to a different location. In other words, he is looking at them from a different angle.

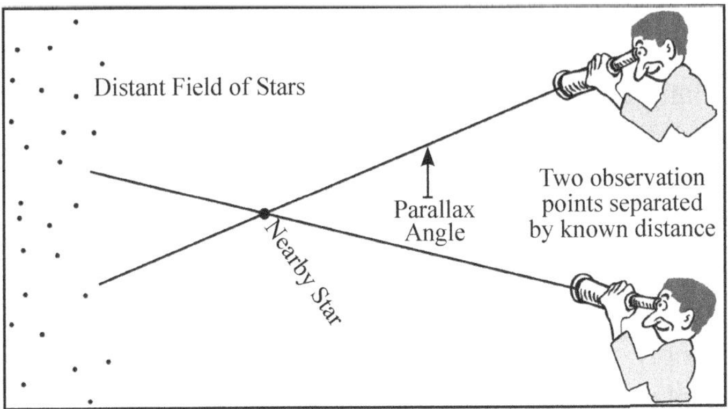

Simplified illustration of Stellar Parallax as calculated by astronomers.

By measuring the angle, scientists can calculate distance. There is one very large obstacle when calculating stellar distance. Most stars are very far away, making the angle so narrow that it is impossible to measure accurately.

In an attempt to obtain a wider angle, astronomers take measurements on both extremes of Earth's orbit around the Sun which allows for a triangular base of about one hundred and eighty six million miles. Now, one hundred and eighty six million miles sounds like quite a base but not when we consider the distance to the most distant stars. A star only hundreds of light years away would result in an angle similar to that observed by two surveyors in New York standing a few feet apart and focusing on a dot in Los Angeles. Quite a narrow angle!

The bottom line is that the distance of far away stars and galaxies is only an educated guess. There are many other methods, but ultimately, all we have to go on is the approximation of scientists.

RIVES THEORY OF RELATIVITY

Many astronomers use the terms Light Year, Parsec, and Astronomical Unit as if they are understood by everyone. But how many people really know what a Parsec is? How many people fully grasp that a Light Year is the distance light would travel (at 12 million miles a minute) after an entire year? A Parsec, very simply, is the parallax of one second of arc. Try explaining that one to the average 8 year old.

Almost everyone has heard of Einstein's theory of Relativity, $E=mc^2$. Well, that's a little too complicated to outline in this volume—so, what I would like to do is introduce to you my theory, which we will call The Rives Theory of Relativity:

IF YOUR RELATIVES CAN'T UNDERSTAND WHAT YOU ARE TALKING ABOUT, YOU NEED TO USE SIMPLER TERMS!

Another aspect of The Rives Theory of Relativity is:

RELATIVE TO THE SPEED OF OUR FASTEST SPACECRAFT, WE CAN DETERMINE HOW LONG IT WOULD TAKE TO REACH AN OBJECT IN SPACE.

Voyager - Launched in 1977 to study the planetary systems of Jupiter and Saturn - expected to push through the heliosheath in deep space.

This simplifies distances. Just as we all know that going 60 miles an hour, we can arrive at a destination 60 miles away in one hour; we can determine how long it would take us to reach objects in space traveling at the speed of our fastest spacecraft—40,000 miles per hour.

Outside of the Solar System, our closest star is in the Alpha Centauri group. It is a very small star known as Proxima Centauri about 4.2 light years away. Just how far is that? In order to better understand just how far that is, let's simplify that distance using the Rives Theory of Relativity: Relative to the speed of our fastest spacecraft, 40,000 miles per hour, it would take us an amazing 70,000 years to reach our closest star!

How long would it take us to reach our closest galaxy? Forty-eight billion years. Deep Sky objects? Hundreds of billions of years. Barely a glimpse at the grandeur of the Universe!

WONDERS WITHOUT NUMBER

Would you be surprised if I told you that there was a common item found in most offices, kitchens, and cafes that could be used to illustrate the grandeur of our Universe? What if I told you that the item I am referring to is a simple coffee-stirrer?

If you were to take a coffee-stirrer outside on a clear night, hold it at arm's length and point it into the sky, the tiny portion of sky you see through the middle is roughly the equivalent of the Hubble Space Telescope HUDF camera's field of view.

In 2003/2004, the HUDF (Hubble Ultra-Deep-Field) camera was employed to photograph a portion of space. A dark area in the constellation Fornax (Southern Hemisphere) was chosen, having few nearby stars. A very long exposure was required to try and bring out extremely faint objects, and over the course of 4 months, the Hubble Telescope collected a cumulative 11 DAY EXPOSURE!

A typical photo taken with a camera in daylight could be 1/100th of a second, while in Earth-bound astrophotography, an average single exposure might be 5 minutes. Imagine the light that could be gathered over approximately 11 DAYS! Once the photos were taken, careful processing was required so that the final result could be viewed.

The completed photograph was nothing less than breathtaking. What would appear to be a dark spot in the sky to a casual observer contained 10,000 galaxies! NOT STARS—GALAXIES, each containing billions of stars!

Great things past finding out, yea, and WONDERS WITHOUT NUMBER

Hubble Space Telescope's Ultra-Deep Field Image. Photograph shows ten thousand galaxies in 3 arcminutes.

WHO IS MESSIER?

Picking up an astronomy magazine, one might find a photo of the gorgeous Messier 42 or come across the spectacular Messier 13. Search the web for galaxies, and you might see Messier 101 or come across Messier 51. But what is this Messier, and what does it mean?

Charles Messier was a Frenchman who lived from 1730 to 1817. Born in Badonviller, France, he was the tenth of twelve children. He discovered his love for astronomy with the appearance of what is known as the six tailed comet of 1744.

In 1751, Messier enlisted in the Navy, under the direction of Joseph Nicolas Delisle who was the resident astronomer at the time. Delisle instructed Messier to keep records of his observations. The first of these observations was that of the transit of Mercury across the face of the Sun in 1753.

Joseph Nicolas Delisle
French Astronomer
1688-1768

Messier's most notable accomplishment was his compilation of a catalogue of over one hundred astronomical objects that, through his small refracting telescope, appeared to be more than just a single star.

The designations M1 to M110, as catalogued by Messier and his colleagues, are still in use today. The catalogue is not organized by object type or by location. Nonetheless, the Messier catalogue comprises nearly all of the most spectacular examples of the five types of deep sky objects: Diffuse Nebulae, Planetary Nebulae, Open Clusters, Globular Clusters, and Galaxies.

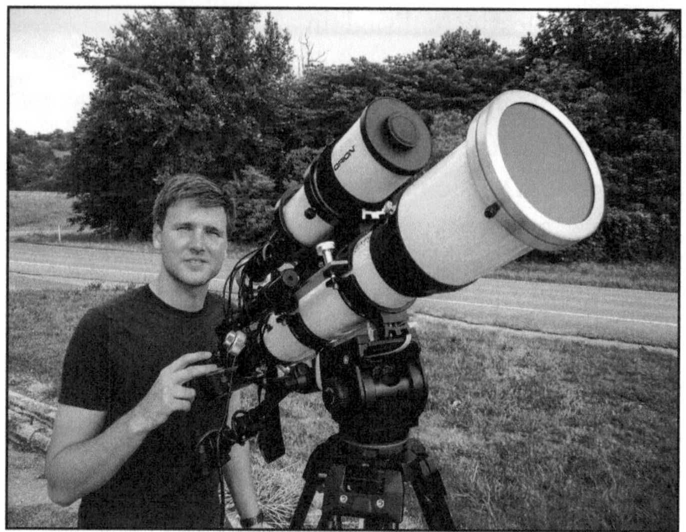

David Rives - Solar observations with Apochromatic Refractor

Today, through the use of highly advanced astronomical equipment, we can observe these breathtaking creations in extreme detail. The apostle Paul tells us: "The invisible things of him from the creation of the world are clearly seen, being understood by the things that are made, even his eternal power and Godhead...."

As I use sophisticated telescopes and technologically advanced imaging systems to view the incredible majesty of the heavens, it leaves me in awe of the amazing designs of our Creator.

> *"Great things past finding out; yea, and wonders without number" —Job 9:10*

MESSIER 1:

Situated within the constellation Taurus, the Crab Nebula, also known as Messier 1, was the very first of 110 objects to be catalogued by Charles Messier. Upon first observation, he mistook this nebula for a comet. This colorful nebula is quite bright and fairly easy to spot using a moderately powerful telescope. It is an interesting deep sky object because of its unique history.

The Crab Nebula is believed to be the result of a giant supernova or exploding star. The event was witnessed and recorded by Chinese and Arab astronomers on July 4, 1054 A.D. The explosion was so bright, reports indicate that it could be seen for weeks in the daylight hours. Today, scientists tell us that the nebula is expanding at a rate of almost 1,000 miles per second.

The nebular shape was first discovered by the English doctor and astronomer John Bevis in 1731. It was placed in the Messier catalog in 1758. The origin of its name "Crab Nebula" comes from The Earl of Rosse observing and making a drawing of the nebula which looked like a crab.

The central star in M1 is a good example of a pulsar, which emits a powerful pulse of radiation once every 33 milliseconds. The variety of stars that we can see and study is simply amazing. First Corinthians 15:41 tells us that: *"There is one glory of the sun, and another glory of the moon, and another glory of the stars: for one star differeth from another star in glory."*

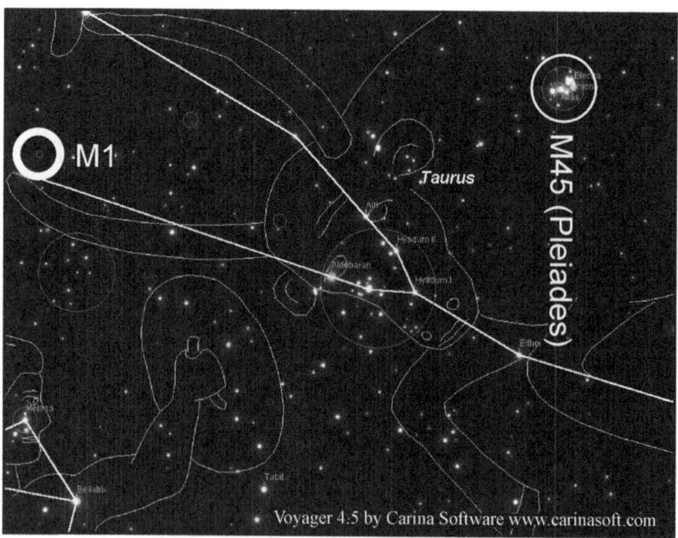

Voyager 4.5 by Carina Software www.carinasoft.com

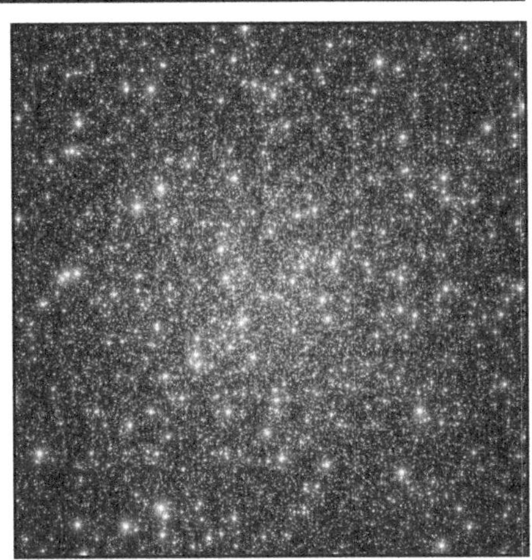

MESSIER 13:
The Great
Hercules Cluster

The Great Hercules Cluster is the most widely recognized globular cluster. It is comprised of hundreds of thousands of stars and is about 25,000 light years away. By way of our fastest spacecraft, it would take 400 million years to reach those stars.

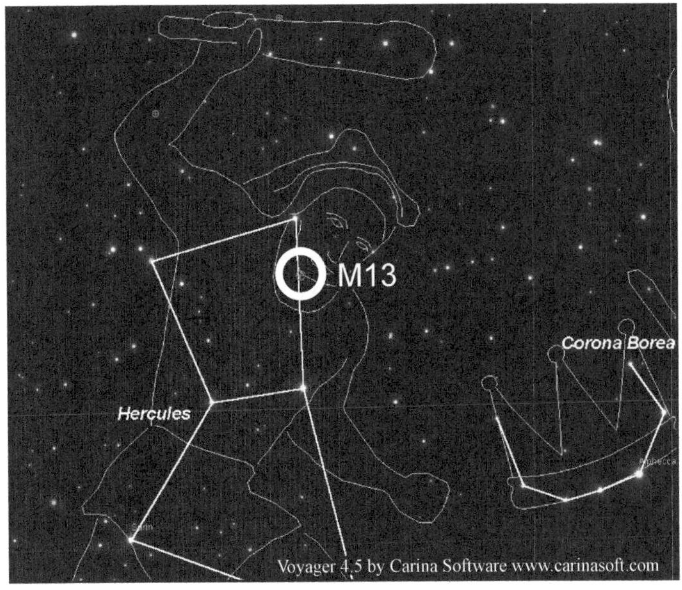

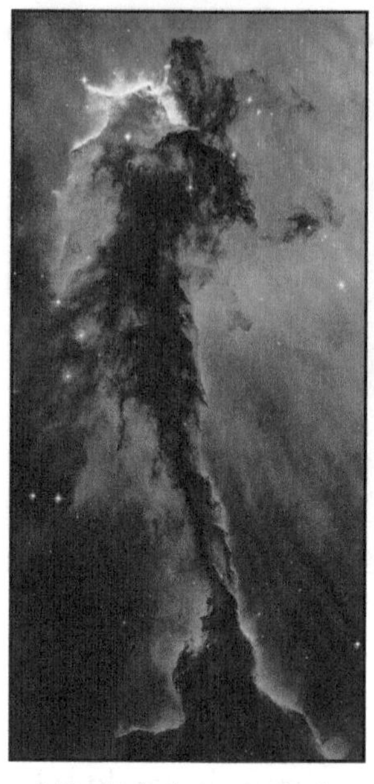

MESSIER 16:

M16—The Eagle Nebula is an emission nebula located within the constellation Serpens. It was first discovered by De Chesaux in 1745, and in 1764, Charles Messier mentioned that the stars were "enmeshed in a faint glow". The astronomer E. E. Barnard (1857-1923) of Nashville, Tennessee, was one of the first to photograph the Eagle Nebula. It is about 7,000 light years from Earth, so based on the Rives Theory of Relativity—relative to our fastest space probes—it would take 117 million years to reach the Eagle Nebula.

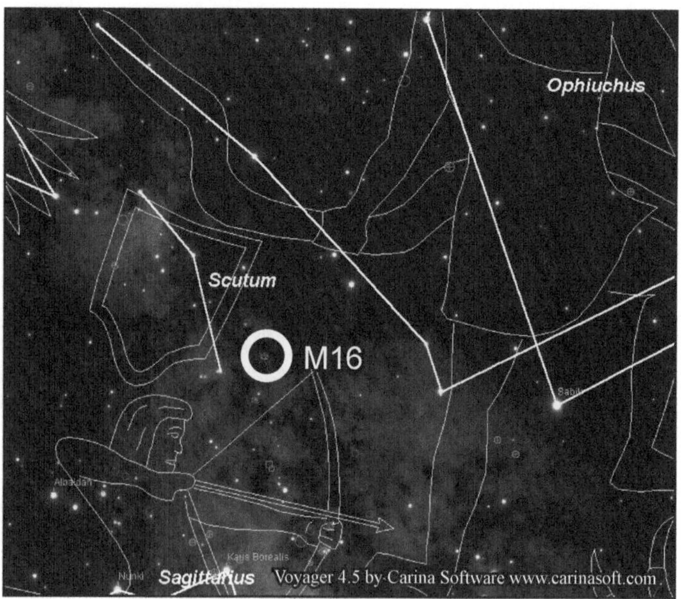

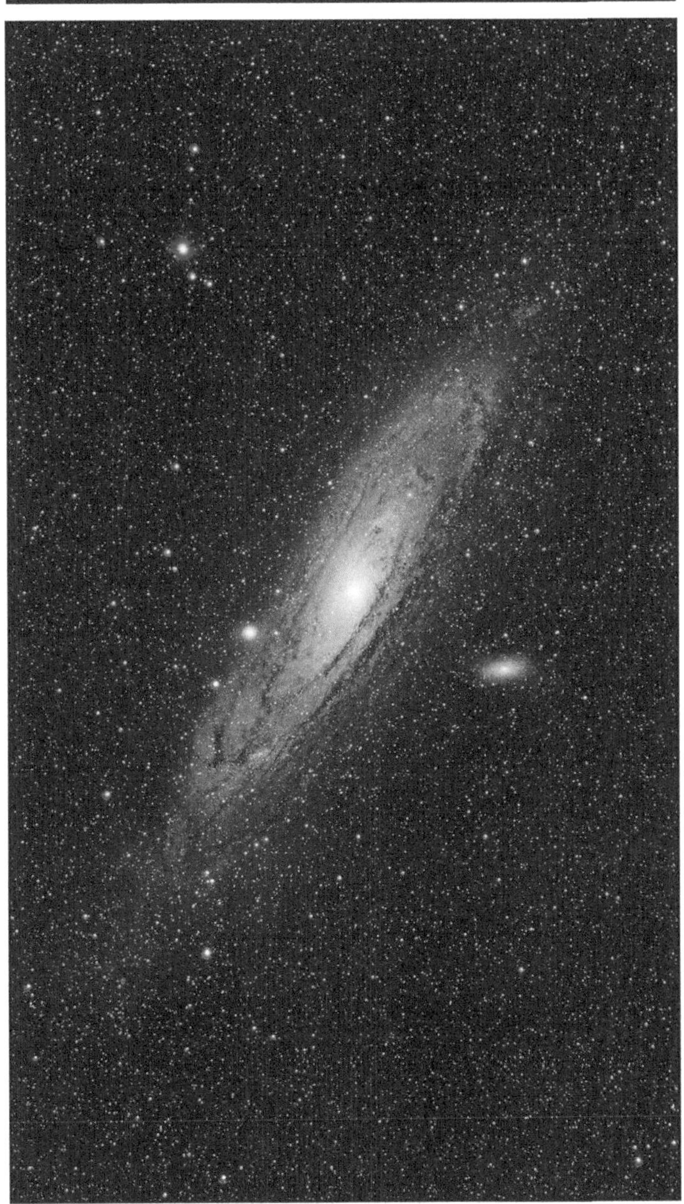

MESSIER 31:
Messier 31—The Andromeda Galaxy

At an estimated 2.5 million light years away, Andromeda is our closest galaxy. It is known as our sister galaxy and contains over 1 trillion stars. It was first recorded in 905 A.D. by the Persian astronomer Abd Al-Rahman Al-Sufi. Using the Rives Theory of Relativity, (that is, travelling at 40,000 MPH) it would take us 48 billion years to reach the Andromeda Galaxy.

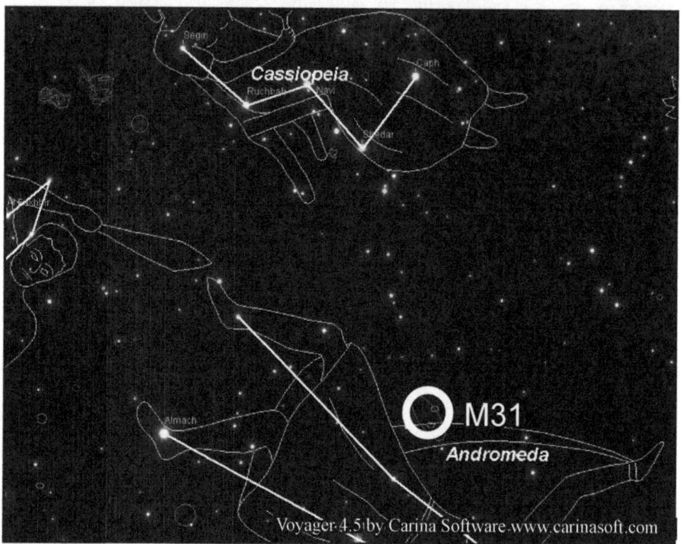

MESSIER 51:

Situated in the constellation Canes Venatici, we find the breathtaking Whirlpool Galaxy, also known as M51. *(See Pg. 105 Star Chart for location of Whirlpool Galaxy)*

This stunning object in the night sky appears as one large spiral galaxy feeding into another much smaller one. The primary galaxy was discovered by Charles Messier in 1774; however, its companion galaxy was not discovered until 1781 by Pierre Mechain.

In 1845, M51 became the first celestial object to be recognized as a spiral shape. Previously, telescopes, with enough optical precision to resolve this, were not yet available. The Whirlpool is the brightest of the Messier 51 group of galaxies, which also includes the Sunflower Galaxy, NGC 5023 and 5229.

A supernova is a rare event to witness, even given the incredible number of stars that are visible in the Universe. This powerful force of a star exploding causes a bright display visible from great distances.

On May 31, 2011, a new supernova was spotted in M51. Using a large 16" telescope, I was able to take photographs of the star going supernova. The photo *(See Pg. 26 for photo)* reveals what the telescope was able to capture with the supernova highlighted. This is an amazing 380 billion years away, travelling at the speed of our fastest spacecraft!

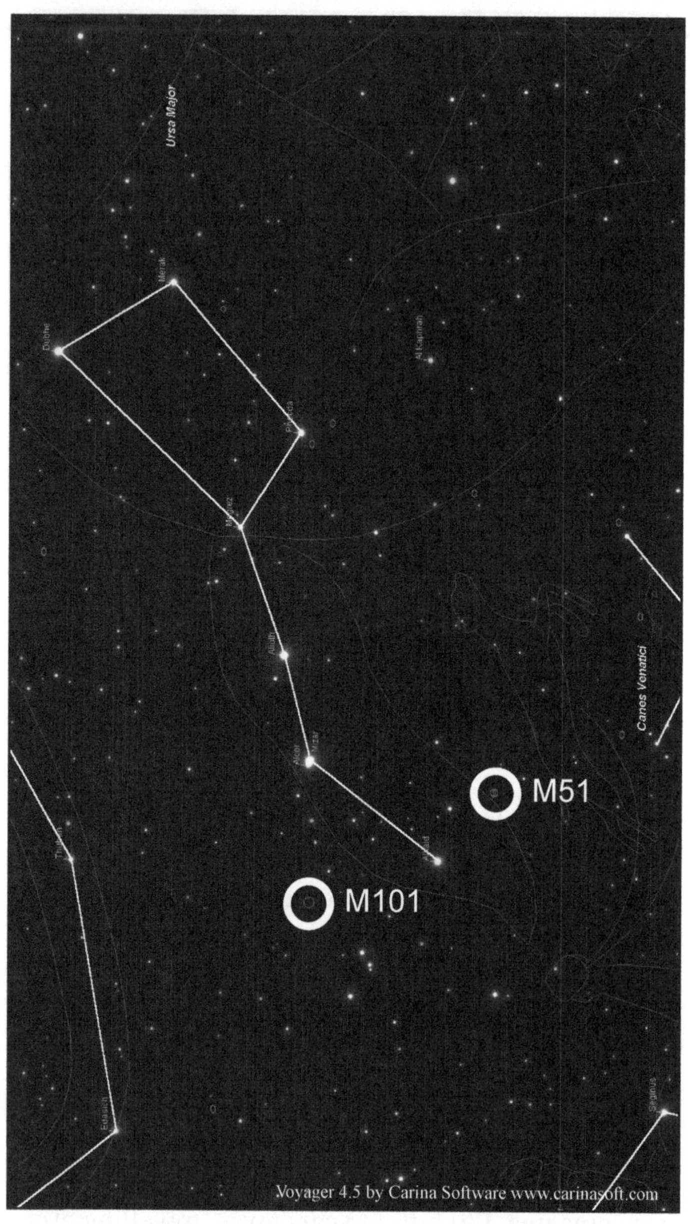

Location of Whirlpool Galaxy (M51), and Pinwheel Galaxy (M101). Outlined is the famous "Big Dipper" portion of Ursa Major

MESSIER 57:
The Ring Nebula

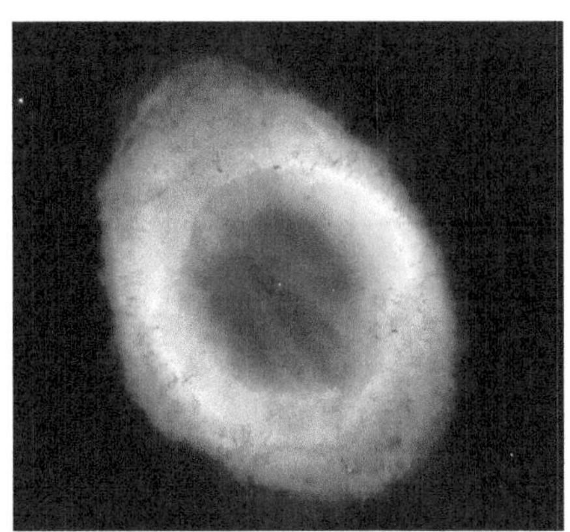

In the constellation Lyra, we find M57, the Ring Nebula. British astronomer and composer William Herschel was known as "The King's Astronomer". He described M57 as a ring of stars. Based on the current rate of expansion, some scientists believe that the appearance of the Ring Nebula might have been around 6,000 years ago. According to the Genesis account, Creation took place around 6,000 years ago, making M57 quite an interesting "coincidence".

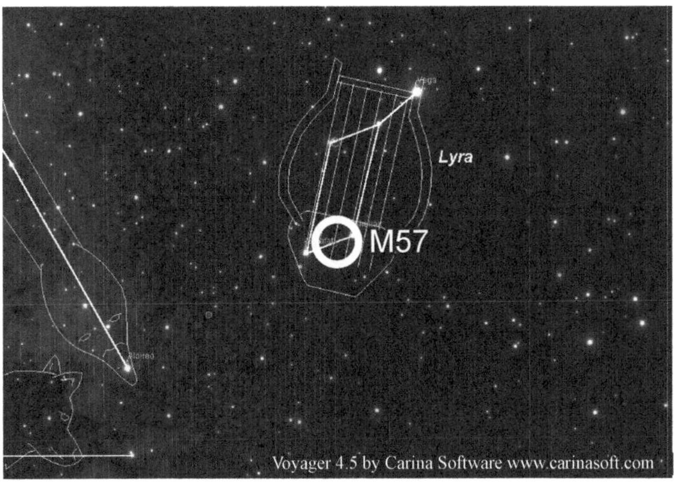

MESSIER 82:

M82, the Cigar Galaxy, is an irregular galaxy located in the constellation Ursa Major, where we also find the famed "Big Dipper". The galaxy is extremely bright in infrared light. In fact, it is the brightest infrared galaxy in the entire sky. The Cigar Galaxy is approximately 12 million light years from Earth and would take over 200 billion years to reach—travelling at 40,000 MPH!

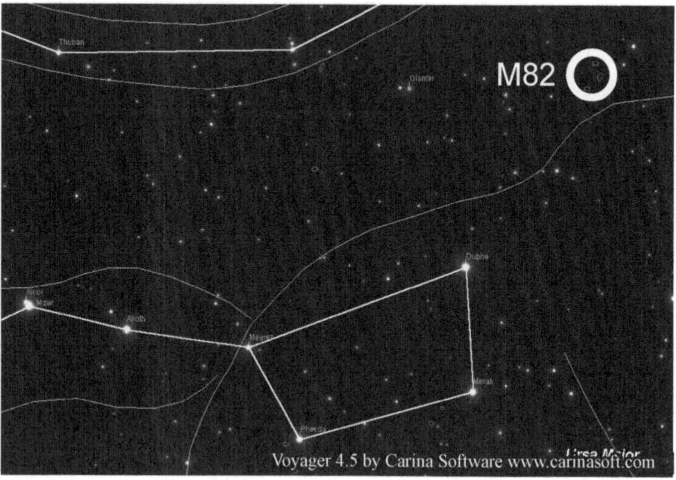

MESSIER 101:

M101, the Pinwheel Galaxy. Perhaps one of the most recognized constellations in the night is Ursa Major, with its easy to find "Big Dipper" *(See Pg. 105 for Star Chart)*. Within this region of bright stars, we find the spiral galaxy known as Messier 101 or the Pinwheel Galaxy.

While it takes a fairly large telescope, as well as dark skies, to view, the Pinwheel is quite an impressive galaxy. M101 was first discovered by the French astronomer and surveyor Pierre Mechain in 1781, who later reported his findings to Charles Messier. Charles Messier added the galaxy as the 101st object to his famous catalogue, thus the title: Messier 101 or M101.

The Pinwheel Galaxy is very large—believed to be twice the size of our own Milky Way. At an estimated

25 million light years away, a trip to M101 would take over 400 billion years, even travelling at the speed of our fastest spacecraft.

In photographs of this beautiful creation, we notice that the Pinwheel's rings are not symmetrical all the way around the nucleus or center of the galaxy. Some people believe that the close proximity of nearby galaxy NGC 5474 may be playing a part in the asymmetrical shape of the Pinwheel due to its gravitational pull.

MESSIER 104:

M104, the Sombrero Galaxy was discovered in 1781 by Pierre Mechain, and it was the first Messier object not listed in the original catalogue. Charles Messier listed one hundred and three objects in his catalogue, and it was only later that M104 was added. It has a very unique structure consisting of a dark dust lane, giving the appearance of a hat brim, and spiral arms, which are clearly visible in other photographs.

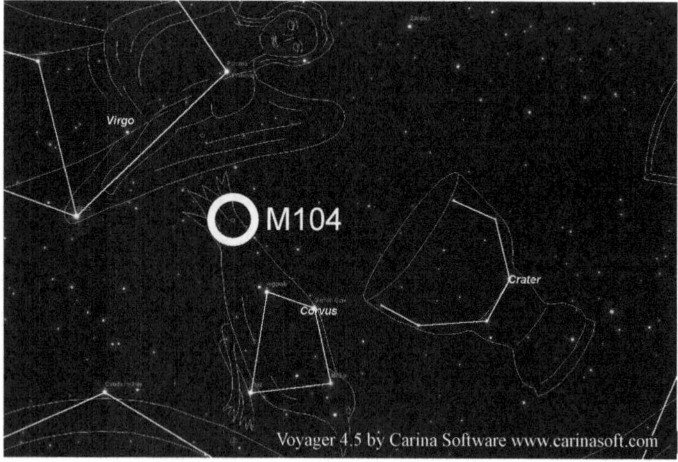

M104, Often referred to as the Sombrero Galaxy because of its similarity to a wide-brimmed hat.

The distance to M104 is about 29 million light years, and using the Rives Theory of Relativity, it would take nearly 500 billion years to reach from Earth.
Sort of puts new meaning to the phrase "A long time ago, in a galaxy far, far away...," doesn't it?

WONDERS WITHOUT NUMBER

The unique celestial objects that we have discussed in this chapter are just a few examples of the creative power of God in the vast expanse of His Universe.

Many have said that these grand formations are the result of billions of years of chance and that Earth is just a tiny speck of debris, floating in an endless mass of chaotic waste. A thorough examination, however, reveals that the cosmic wonders of deep space are full of order and design. Our tiny planet is infinitely more special, for...

> ***"God so loved the world that He gave His only begotten Son, that whosoever believeth in him should not perish, but have everlasting life." —John 3:16***

Chapter Eight
Astronomy, Astrology and Mythology

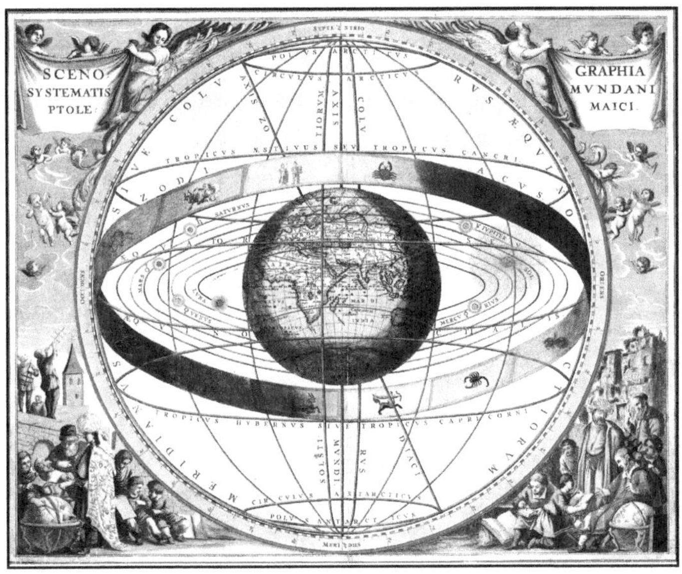

The Genesis account tells us that the lights in the heavens are to be for signs. That is not to be confused with the astrology condemned by the Bible as pagan in nature. Did the constellations that are now presented as mythological objects originally have a purer, Biblical meaning?

"Canst thou bind the sweet influences of Pleiades, or loose the bands of Orion? Canst thou bring forth Mazzaroth in his season?" —Job 38:31

The meaning of the Hebrew word translated 'Mazzaroth' is a subject of debate. Some Biblical scholars believe that Mazzaroth is actually a reference to the divisions of the constellations along the celestial sphere.

It has been proposed that the Mazzaroth was originally given as a prophetic guide to the coming of Messiah, a story spelled out in the heavens that was later corrupted by the interpretations of astrologers, those who believe that the alignment of celestial bodies actually influence human destiny.

The zodiac in use during the time of the Roman Empire was thought to have been inherited from the Babylonians. They divided the circle of constellations into 12 equal parts, corresponding with the month of the year.

THE ZODIAC

Ptolemy, a 2nd century Greek astronomer, described the divisions of the constellations by their Latin names. The term Zodiac actually means "Circle of Animals".

It is very important to consider the fact that the constellations vary in size. They don't accurately represent 12 equal divisions of the year. In addition, astronomers now recognize a 13th constellation along the ecliptic, the constellation Ophiucus.

An astronomical phenomenon, known as precession of the equinox, proves the predictions of astrologers to be without basis. Due to precession since Babylonian times, the sign of Aries is actually within the constellation Pisces.

THE CALENDAR AND ASTRONOMY

Based on the Zodiac, the movements of the heavens became a means of divination. In ancient times, celestial bodies such as the Sun, Moon, and stars were considered to be gods and goddesses. They became the central figures of the Zodiac.

Scripture informs us that they worshipped the <u>created</u> more than the Creator. In the book of Kings, Josiah ordered that those who worshipped the Sun, the Moon, Mazzaloth, and all the host of heaven be put to death.

Idolatry was never an acceptable alternative to the Biblically prescribed worship of the Creator. Earlier, at the time of the Exodus, the image of a golden calf was worshipped. That sin resulted in the death of three thousand people.

Much can be learned about the significance of lights in the heavens from the Hebrew luni-solar calendar. The beginning of months is determined by the observation of the Moon. The Feasts of the Lord, including Passover, are based heavily on lunar timing. Days, seasons, and years are calculated by the position of the Sun and Moon, as well as the stars.

Our present calendar does not coincide with that used in Biblical times. It is a solar calendar adopted by Pope Gregory in 1582. Many of the months are named after pagan gods, the very same mythological gods acknowledged by astrologers. Not only that, but our days of the week are named after pagan gods associated with astrological symbols.

Scripture informs us *(Genesis 1:14)* that the Sun, Moon, and stars were created for signs, seasons, days, and years. Thousands of years have passed, but just as in the beginning, those very same heavenly bodies can still be relied upon for our calculation of time.

PIRATES OF THE MEDITERRANEAN

Around the 1st and 2nd centuries before the time of Christ, Rome was in a power-struggle with their neighbors. Pirates, from the area of Cilicia, were rising in strength and attacking trade ships that carried goods across the Mediterranean.

The historian Plutarch describes the gravity of the situation like this: "While the Romans were embroiled in civil wars at the gates of Rome, the sea was left unguarded...The ships of the pirates numbered more than a thousand, and the cities captured by them four hundred."

The chaos they created was not limited to the sea. These Pirates of the Mediterranean, according to Plutarch, practiced "certain secret rites, among which, those of Mithras continue to the present time, having been first instituted by them."

THE MYSTERY GOD MITHRA

Mithra, was regarded as a deity of the sun, and the secret cult worshipped the heavenly bodies found in astrology. Pagan mythology encouraged the worship of idols created by man. The Bible, however, calls for the worship of the Creator of the Universe.

The author standing at the Temple of Hercules in Ostia Antica, Italy

On one of my trips to Italy, I had the opportunity to visit the ancient Roman seaport at Ostia Antica. The historical remains of Ostia are located about 30 kilometers from the city of Rome on the shores of the Mediterranean. Once the bustling seaport for all of Rome's trade and industry, today, much of this important town still remains.

Over the years, the Mediterranean has receded, making the port inaccessible to ships, but walking down the Decumanus, or stepping into the ruins of the temple of Hercules, it is easy to imagine what it would have looked like in its day.

Decumanus Maximus
Main Street / East-West

Scattered through the city are dozens of well-preserved Mithraeums, worship areas for the Persian mystery god Mithra. In one Mithraeum, the deity is displayed on the far wall, while stone benches line the right and left sides.

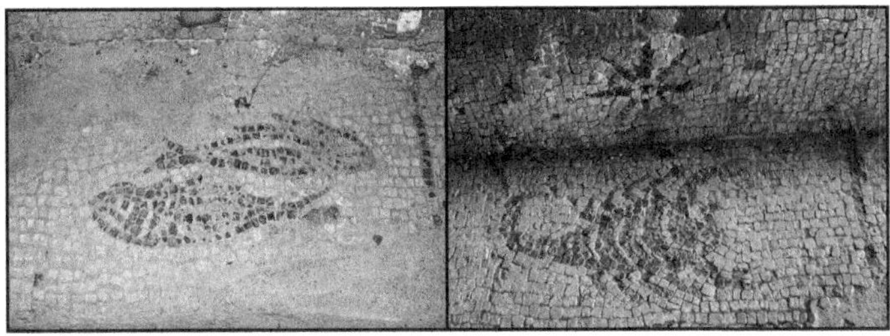

A look at the symbolism portrayed along the benches reveals representations of the astrological signs of the Zodiac: Scorpio, Virgo, Pisces, etcetera. As the focal point of the Mithraeum, we find the stone plaque of Mithra himself—the god of the Sun, flanked by the Moon and stars.

The author standing in a Mithraeum - A worship place of the secret cult. Astrological symbolism can be found all over the room

Mithra Slaying the bull with iconic representations of the moon, stars, Scorpio, Hydra, Canis, and Taurus. Mithra himself represents the Sun.

The Bible makes it clear:

> ***"Take ye therefore good heed ...lest thou lift up thine eyes unto heaven, and when thou seest the sun, and the moon, and the stars, even all the host of heaven, shouldest be driven to worship them."***
>
> ***—Deuteronomy 4:15-19***

ORION, THE GREAT HUNTER

According to Greek mythology, Orion was known to be the son of Poseidon, the god of the sea. During the course of his fabled hunting expeditions, Orion threatened to kill all the living animals. Orion was subsequently killed himself by a giant scorpion. After his death, we're told that Zeus placed Orion in the sky as a constellation, becoming enshrined in the sky as "The Great Hunter".

Left: Hesiod and the Muse - Gustave Moreau 1891
Center: Diana and the body of Orion - Daniel Seiter 1685
Right: Homer and His Guide - William-Adolphe Bouguereau 1874

In ancient literature, Homer and Hesiod refer to Orion as an important constellation which, along with the Sun, was used to determine the beginning of years. The constellation Orion was known by the Syrians as Al Jabar or the Giant and by the Chaldeans as Tammuz, which the book of Ezekiel associates with the idolatry that plagued the nation of Israel.

As the belt stars of the constellation Orion rose above the horizon just before sunrise, the Chaldeans began their month of Tammuz. Today, Tammuz is the fourth month on the Jewish calendar.

ORION AND THE HEBREW WORD KESIYL

The English word "Orion" as found in our Bibles comes from the Hebrew word כסיל (kes-eel). The book of Job speaks of Arcturus, Orion, the Pleiades, and the chambers of the south.

In Job 9, we read of He *"Which alone spreadeth out the heavens, and treadeth upon the waves of the sea, which maketh Arcturus, Orion, and Pleiades, and the chambers of the south, which doeth great things past finding out; yea, and wonders without number." —Job 9:10*

Again in Job 38, the Creator asks Job if he is able to *"loose the bands of Orion"*. Basically, he was being challenged: Can you loosen Orion's belt?

In the book of Amos, Israel was instructed to *"Seek him that maketh the seven stars and Orion, and turneth the shadow of death into the morning, and maketh the day dark with night" —Amos 5:8*

In the book of Ezekiel, Tammuz, the pagan god associated with Orion, is mentioned in reference to the idolatry being practiced by the house of Israel:

"Then he brought me to the door of the gate of the LORD'S house...and, behold, there sat women weeping for Tammuz. Then said he unto me, "Hast thou seen this, O son of man? Is it a light thing to the house of Judah that they commit the abominations which they commit here?" —Ezekiel 8:14-15

Through the imaginations of men, the *"created"* had come to be worshipped more than the Creator Himself. They had *changed the truth of God into a lie.* The God of the Bible is a *jealous god*, and he will not allow the association of pagan ritual with His worship.

> *"For the wrath of God is revealed from heaven against all ungodliness and unrighteousness of men, who hold the truth in unrighteousness; Because that which may be known of God is manifest in them; for God hath shewed it unto them. For the invisible things of him from the creation of the world are clearly seen, being understood by the things that are made, even his eternal power and Godhead; so that they are without excuse: Because that, when they knew God, they glorified him not as God, neither were thankful; but became vain in their imaginations, and their foolish heart was darkened. Professing themselves to be wise, they became fools, And changed the glory of the uncorruptible God into an image made like to corruptible man, and to birds, and fourfooted beasts, and creeping things. Wherefore God also gave them up to uncleanness through the lusts of their own hearts, to dishonour their own bodies between themselves: Who changed the truth of God into a lie, and worshipped and served the creature more than the Creator, who is blessed for ever. Amen." —Romans 1:18-25*

As we witness the grandeur of the Universe, let us seek our Creator, Jesus Christ: All things were created by Him and for Him. "*He was in the world, and the world was made by him, and the world knew him not. He came unto his own, and his own received him not. But as many as received Him, to them gave he power to become the sons of God, even to them that believe on his name." —John 1:10-12*

The Great Orion Nebula - Photo by David Rives

THE GREAT ORION NEBULA, BETELGEUSE, AND RIGEL

Within the constellation Orion lies the most notable nebula in the sky, the Great Orion Nebula. By way of a refracting telescope, the nebula is thought to have been first observed by French astronomer Nicolas-Claude Fabri de Peiresc in 1610. Under dark skies, the nebula can be seen with the naked eye as a bright glow near the central star of Orion's sword. The bright core stars of the nebula are known as the Trapezium, from which magnificent clouds of gas spread out for some 15 light years in every direction.

The famous "Trapezium" a bright cluster of four stars forming a trapezoid shape. Located in the center of the Great Orion Nebula, the "Trapezium" illuminates the surrounding gases.

Betelgeuse and Rigel are the brightest stars in the constellation Orion. They are easily seen above and below the famous belt and sword.

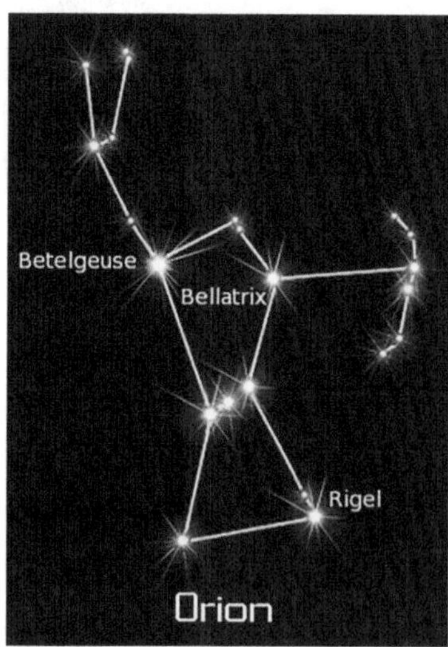

Betelgeuse, the ninth brightest star in the sky, is a red supergiant. As one of the largest known stars, Betelgeuse is truly a giant—estimated at over 15 times more massive than our Sun and 1,000 times its diameter. Betelgeuse is so large that it could contain over one and a half billion of our suns. If placed in the center of our Solar System, the outer surface of Betelgeuse would extend almost to the orbit of Jupiter—engulfing Mercury, Venus, Mars, and the Earth.

Marking the heel of Orion, we find the blue white star Rigel, the 7th brightest star in the sky.

Estimated at 900 light years away, Rigel, also considered a supergiant, is 50,000 times brighter than our Sun. What we see with the naked eye is actually two stars, a binary system, and is composed of one very large, super-bright star and a small, fainter star only observable by larger telescopes.

The light from Rigel illuminates a nearby reflection nebula sometimes called the Witch Head Nebula because of its peculiar shape that resembles a fairy tale

witch. The blue color of the nebula is not only a result of reflected blue light from Rigel, but is also due to the fact that the dust particles that make up the nebula are thought to reflect blue light more than red. Have you ever wondered why our daytime sky is blue? It's for a similar reason. Molecules in our atmosphere scatter blue light more than red.

How far away, on average, are the stars of Orion? Scientists are really not sure. They estimate the distance at over 600 light years. Traveling at the speed of our fastest spacecraft, some 40,000 miles per hour, it would take us over 10 million years to reach the bright stars of Orion.

The book of Isaiah tells us that the LORD created the heavens and stretched them out. The vast Universe gives us just a glimpse of His creative power.

THE SEVEN SISTERS, THE PLEIADES

Most everyone is familiar with the Trojan horse, but you might be asking, "What does the Trojan horse have to do with astronomy?" During the 1st century B.C., Virgil wrote of the Trojan horse and the Trojan wars. The account of the Trojan horse is also found in Homer's Odyssey written around 750 B.C.

Here's the connection: Both Homer and Virgil also wrote of the *Pleiades* or the Seven Sisters, that famous star cluster in the constellation Taurus.

Although Homer was the first to mention the *Pleiades* in Western culture, long before that time, the Bible speaks of the *Pleiades* in *Amos 5, Job 38, and Job 9.*

> ***"How should man be just with God? If he will contend with him, he cannot answer him one of a thousand. Which commandeth the sun, and it riseth not;***

and sealeth up the stars. Which alone spreadeth out the heavens, and treadeth upon the waves of the sea. Which maketh Arcturus, Orion, and Pleiades, and the chambers of the south. Which doeth great things past finding out; yea, and wonders without number."

—Job 9:1-10

Located within the constellation Taurus, the Pleiades may be the most noticeable star cluster in the sky. Lying within the plane of our own galaxy, the cluster contains over 500 stars. Seven of them are easily visible with the naked eye. In Greek mythology, the central stars were known as the Seven Sisters, or the daughters of Zeus, and were pursued by the nearby constellation Orion.

Surrounding the bright stars, a reflection nebula creates a beautiful blue glow when viewed through a telescope.

The Pleiades are about 440 light years from Earth, and using the Rives Theory of Relativity [That is, relative to our fastest spacecraft travelling 40,000 MPH], it would take seven million years just to reach the Pleiades.

SIRIUS AND THE "DOG DAYS OF SUMMER"

Also known as the 'Dog Star', Sirius is thought to be 8.6 light years away. It is actually a binary or double-star system, composed of the primary star Sirius A and the faint Sirius B beside it. Some observers refer to these two as Sirius and his pup.

The hottest part of the year, known by the ancients as "the dog days of summer," was known by the Greeks to begin at the rising of Sirius, the dog star. In Greek, Σείριος "seirios" means "glowing".

Apotheosis of Homer - Jean Auguste Dominique Ingres, 1827

Homer's <u>Iliad</u> relates Achilles' journey to Troy on a summer night with Sirius rising in the sky.

One ancient astronomer dating back to the first century, describes the star as red, leaving many astronomers confused with current observations. While this description may have been a simple error, several other ancient references have been noted accounting a red Sirius and some describing a blue star. Whether or not the apparent color has changed over time, today, Sirius is a very bright white main sequence star.

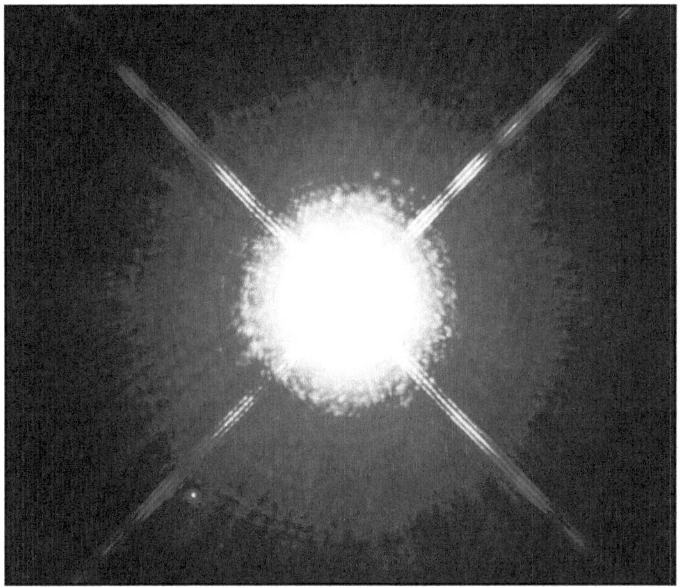

At 8 light years away, Sirius has a magnitude of -1.4, making it (besides our Sun) the brightest appearing star in the heavens. It is easily seen just to the northeast of the Constellation Orion.

SOTHIS – HAPPY NEW YEAR?

In the summer months, the ancient Egyptians recognized that the rising of Sothis, or Sirius, just before dawn, marked the time of year when the Nile

River would begin to overflow. As an agricultural civilization, the overflowing Nile brought fertile soil to the land of Egypt, making it a very important time of year: This was so important that the rising of Sirius marked the beginning of the Egyptian New Year.

It turns out that the rising of the star Sirius is a good indicator of a Sidereal Year. Scientists define a sidereal year as the time it takes the Earth to revolve once around the Sun, relative to other stars: 365.256 days. It just so happens that the rising of Sirius from year to year, known as a 'Sothic Cycle', is almost exactly 365.25 days in duration.

A document known as the Canopus Decree, or the table of Tanis, proclaimed a five-day national festival at the rising of Sothis in honor of Ptolemy III, his queen, and the "Benefactory Gods". The decree was written in Greek, Demotic, and in Hieroglyphics, making it an important key in deciphering hieroglyphic inscriptions.

"Thus saith the LORD, Learn not the way of the heathen, and be not dismayed at the signs of heaven; for the heathen are dismayed at them. For the customs of the people are vain..."—Jeremiah 10:2-3

CHAPTER NINE
THE FOUNDATION OF OUR FAITH

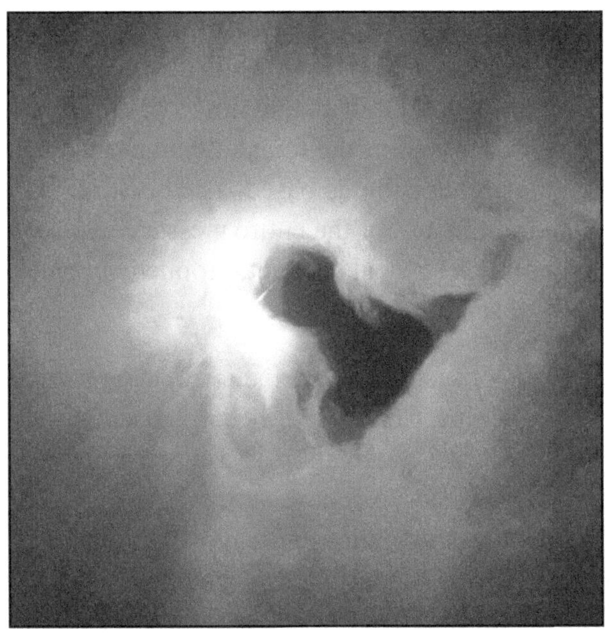

If the foundations be destroyed, what can the righteous do?
—Psalm 11:3

"If the foundations be destroyed, what can the righteous do?" Today more than ever, this question calls our attention to the dangers of an ever increasing attack on the foundations of our faith—the very first sentence in the Bible. *"In the beginning, God created the heaven and the earth." Genesis 1:1*

Jesus Christ plainly taught that the writings of Moses were to be received as fact; yet, in opposition to the words of the Creator Himself, unproven theories of evolution, presented as fact by our schools and universities, challenge the reliability of scripture. While Christianity looks on with little concern, the religion of evolution, in an attempt to destroy the faith of believers, questions the foundational principal upon which the whole Bible is based. The book of Genesis lays the foundation for the entire message of scripture, including the historical account, prophetic events, and the way of salvation.

After years of secular indoctrination, a large number of those professing Christ have been persuaded that the Genesis account of Creation is a mere fable, a fairy tale, or an allegory. Today, as evolutionists attempt to destroy the foundation by way of gradual erosion, young people are departing from the faith, and church leaders cannot seem to figure out why. What can the righteous do?

Those of us who believe the literal words of scripture must answer the challenge. We must stand firm in our beliefs, unashamed of the fact that we believe what the Bible says.

I believe just as the scriptures state, that "*In the beginning, God created the heaven and earth.*" —Not in billions of years, not in millions of years, not even in thousands of years, but in six literal days. He then blessed the seventh day and hallowed it. The Creation week was complete, and everything was GOOD. This is the original basis for the 7-day week in use today.

The record of Creation was not intended to be subject to scholarly interpretation. It is a plain account of the very beginning.

Every word of God is pure: he is a shield unto them that put their trust in him. Add thou not unto his words, lest he reprove thee, and thou be found a liar. —Proverbs 30:5-6

The Apostle Paul Preaching in Athens - Raphael, 1515

EVOLUTION - MOST FOOLISH NOTION

Charles Spurgeon, often referred to as the Prince of Preachers, said that one day people "will speak, amid roars of laughter, of evolution; and the day will come, when there will not be a child but will look upon it as being the most foolish notion that ever crossed the human mind."

In reference to the proponents of evolution, Spurgeon exclaimed: "The philosophy now in vogue labours to shut God out of his own creation. They inform us that by some means this world and all that is therein were evolved. Even this will not long content the men of progress: they care nothing for evolution in itself, but only so far as it may serve their purpose of escaping from the thought of God."

Today, over one hundred and twenty years after the time of Spurgeon, many pastors are teaching their congregations that aspects of the Bible are not to be taken literally. They would lead us to believe that some passages from the book of Genesis, such as Creation and the global flood, are nothing more than allegorical stories. Why should we be concerned? Can belief in evolution really be such an important issue?

Joseph Stalin, originally raised in the Georgian Orthodox Church, later became an atheist, and believed, as Lenin, that religion needed to be removed in order to establish a communist society. Atheism was advanced by way of public education and anti-religious propaganda.

Stalin was talking with a childhood friend one day when he volunteered a revealing statement: "You know, they are fooling us, there is no God... I'll lend you a book to read; it will show you that the world and all living things are quite different from what you imagine, and all this talk about God is sheer nonsense."

Joseph Stalin, 1878-1953
Soviet Union, General Secretary of the Communist Party

Questioned about the book, Stalin replied:

"Darwin. You must read it."

PIONEERS OF SCIENCE

Today, while evolutionary science questions the Genesis account, that has not always been the case. To many of the greatest minds in science, belief in a Creator was a foundational principle.

Johannes Kepler, 1571-1630

JOHANNES KEPLER: The astronomer Johannes Kepler spent most of his time in Austria, and in Prague, where he pioneered much of the work on planetary motion. Kepler said that God used geometry when he laid out the world so that it might be best and most beautiful and finally most like the Creator.

Kepler became interested in astronomy early in life. At age six, he observed the Great Comet of 1577. Working with his telescopes, he realized that he was witnessing things that had never before been seen. Kepler said, "God himself has waited six thousand years for his work to be seen." He is known to have prayed: "I thank thee my Creator and my Lord, that Thou hast given me this joy in thy Creation, this thrill in the works of Thy hand."

GALILEO GALILEI:

Galileo had great respect for Johannes Kepler. He once told Kepler: "I esteem myself happy to have as great an ally as you in my search for truth."

Galileo (1564-1642) was born in Pisa, Italy, and was known as the father of modern observational astronomy. He was one of the first to employ the now widely-used refracting telescope in astronomy. Using those telescopes, he discovered four of Jupiter's largest moons: Io, Europa, Ganymede, and Callisto.

Stephen Hawking, a modern-day cosmologist and die-hard atheist, admits that "Galileo, perhaps more than any other single person, was responsible for the birth of modern science." Let's take a look at the foundation upon which this brilliant scientist based his findings.

Galileo is said to have stated that "Mathematics is the language with which God has written the universe." In his writings, he explained: "It was well said that... the Holy Scripture cannot err, and that the decrees therein contained are absolutely true."

SIR ISAAC NEWTON:

Sir Isaac Newton, 1642-1727

Sir Isaac Newton was, and still is, a great influence in science. His legendary work on gravity, said to have been spurred by an apple falling from a tree, has become an iconic event in history. What was this great scientist's <u>foundation of faith?</u>

"God created everything by number, weight, and measure."

Quoting Sir Isaac Newton:
"It is the perfection of God's works that they are all done with the greatest simplicity. He is the God of order and not of confusion."

"Truth is ever to be found in simplicity, and not in the multiplicity and confusion of things."

"Gravity explains the motions of the planets, but it cannot explain who set the planets in motion. God governs all things and knows all that is or can be done."

"Atheism is so senseless & odious to mankind that it never had many professors. Can it be by accident that all birds, beasts & men have....just two eyes and no more on either side the face and just two ears on either side the head ....two arms on the shoulders and two legs on the hips, one on either side and no more? Whence arises this uniformity... but from the counsel and contrivance of an Author? Did blind chance know that there was light... and fit the eyes of all creatures after the most curious manner to make use of it? These and such like considerations always have and ever will prevail with man kind to believe that there is a being who made all things and has all things in his power and who is therefore to be feared."

Newton's Laws of Motion contain a well-known principle: "To every action there is always opposed an equal reaction." Let us use the same principle in our faith. With every action taken to remove God from science, let us oppose it with an equal action to ensure that God stays at the forefront of our lives.

BUILDING BLOCKS OF EDUCATION

At the beginning of 20th century, Biblical study was considered to be an important aspect of education. In 1915, the Bible was required reading in most public schools. A legal ordinance in Tennessee directed that 10 verses of the Bible must be read every day.

William Jennings Bryan

In 1923, the first anti-evolution bills were passed in Oklahoma and Florida. Textbooks in Oklahoma were banned for their teaching of the "Materialist Conception of History—the Darwin Theory of Creation". William Jennings Bryan stated that there would be "demoralization involved in accepting a brute ancestry."

In 1925, under the order of the Tennessee legislature, a bill was passed making it a crime "to teach any theory that denies the story of the Divine Creation of man as taught in the Bible, and to teach instead that man had descended from a lower order of animal."

Left: John T. Scopes Dayton, TN teacher

Right: Clarence Darrow Defense Attorney

It was soon after, that the ACLU stepped in, and the summer of '25 saw the beginning of the Scopes Monkey Trial. John T. Scopes, a Dayton, Tennessee, school teacher, was accused of violating the law which made it unlawful to teach evolution in a state-funded school. As prosecutor, William Jennings Bryan argued against the famous defense attorney Clarence Darrow. Scopes was found guilty and fined $100; however, the verdict was later overturned on a technicality.

Less than 100 years later, the view of "Divine Creation," which was highly esteemed in 1925, has been all but eliminated in our public schools. Instead, the religion of evolution is now taught as fact.

As late as the 1940's, evolutionary doctrine was still being censored from textbooks; yet, today, one would do well to find even a casual mention of the Biblical account of Creation. Due to the acceptance of the anti-Biblical theories of Darwinian evolution, the original foundation of education, the belief in a Creator, has crumbled. Genesis gives us an historical account of exactly how we came to be, and it does not involve monkeys losing their tails.

EDUCATIONAL INDOCTRINATION

Today, universities originally established to teach Christian principles now take pride in religious diversity.

HARVARD COLLEGE:

Harvard College was established in 1636. It was named for its first benefactor, John Harvard, a young minister who left his library and a sizeable portion of his estate for the purpose of training Puritan ministers. The University's early motto was "Truth for Christ and the Church". As stated in Harvard's Rules and Precepts: "Let every Student be plainly instructed, and earnestly pressed to consider well, the main end of his life and studies is, to know God and Jesus Christ which is eternal life" and encouraged the use of Christ "as the only foundation of all sound knowledge and learning."

THE ONLY FOUNDATION!

Today, the foundation of learning at Harvard is far from the faith of Christ. They boast that the student body and its faculty come from a variety of religious backgrounds, and the unproven theories of evolution, in opposition to the words of scripture, are presented as fact. A university that was once based upon the infallibility of scripture now places its faith in the wisdom of man.

The theory of evolution is a Creation account directly opposed to the one we find in the book of Genesis—the FOUNDATION upon which our faith is based. While some theologians are more than willing to compromise the truths of scripture, the uncompromising religion of evolution is hard at work attempting to destroy that foundation. By way of vague and rambling metaphysical philosophy, evolutionists insult our Creator while Christianity, for the most part, stands idly by—intimidated by the wisdom of the world.

"It is better to trust in the LORD than to put confidence in man." —Psalm 118:8

YALE UNIVERSITY

YALE UNIVERSITY:
Established in 1701 in an effort to create an institution for clergy, Yale University's coat of arms contains the Biblical phrase "Urim and Thummim" written in Hebrew.

"Urim and Thummim"
Banner: "Light and Truth"

Today, "the Yale Department of Religious Studies provides opportunities for the scholarly study of a number of religious traditions and disciplines...The Department offers a wide array of courses that cover the major religions of the world, with a strong emphasis on their history and their intellectual traditions."

What can the righteous do? We can and must stand for the literal truths of the Bible; in the beginning, a loving Creator formed the Universe in six literal days, and, *behold, it was very good.*

FOUNDING FATHERS

"We hold these truths to be self evident, that all men are created equal, that they are endowed by their Creator with certain unalienable Rights, that among these are Life, Liberty and the pursuit of Happiness."

The Declaration of Independence is undoubtedly the most famous document in American history. The words found in the opening statement mark a critical point in history. More than that, they clearly illustrate that the principles upon which the United States of America were founded include belief in a Creator.

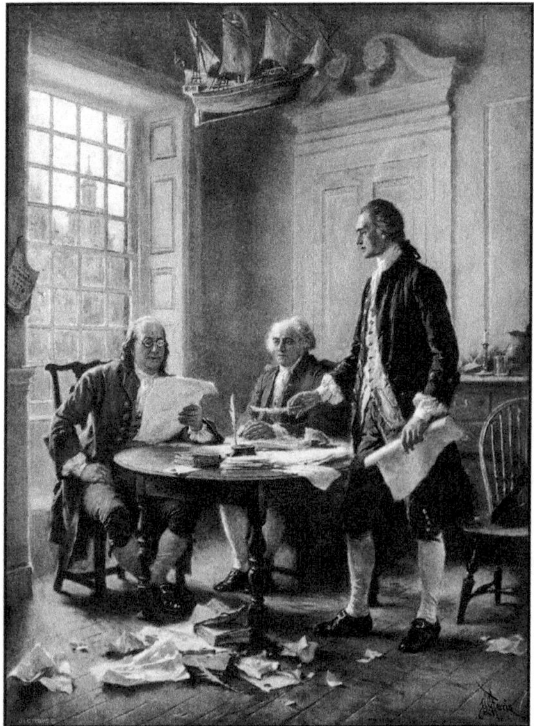

The Committee drafting the Declaration of Independence

Somehow, many people have lost the zeal for God and settled for the religion of chance. America was at its greatest when we had leaders standing in unison with common goals and beliefs; but, as we push farther away from God's plan without Him to guide and direct us, this country stumbles aimlessly and confused towards the brink of peril.

"In the supposed state of nature, all men are equally bound by the laws of nature, or to speak more properly, the laws of the Creator."
—Samuel Adams

It is apparent that the majority of America's founding fathers considered belief in a Creator to be an extremely important aspect of sound government. They believed in, and defended, the right to life and liberty as intended by a loving Creator. They realized that true freedom is not separation *from God*, but, rather, is given *by God*.

Consider the closing statements of the Declaration of Independence: "For the support of this Declaration, with a firm reliance on the protection of Divine Providence, we mutually pledge to each other our Lives, our Fortunes, and our sacred Honor."

"Surely his salvation is nigh them that fear him; that glory may dwell in our land." —Psalm 85:9

PUBLIC OPINION

Things have changed since the time of the founding fathers. A Barna Group article entitled Christianity Is No Longer Americans' Default Faith *(1/12/09, The Barna Group, www.barna.org)* gives us insight into what the general public now believes when it comes to religion. It isn't encouraging...

"Among individuals who describe themselves as Christian...Close to half believe that Satan does not exist...One-third contend that Jesus sinned while He was on earth."

"Leading the charge in the move to customize one's package of beliefs are people under the age of 25, among whom more than four out of five (82%) said they develop their own combination of beliefs..."

"Millions now contend that they will experience eternal salvation because they confessed their sins and accepted Christ as their savior, but also believe that a person can do enough good works to earn eternal salvation"

"Feelings and emotions now play a significant role in the development of people's faith views."

"Today, Americans are more likely to pit a variety of non-Christian options against various Christian-based views. This has resulted in…worldviews based on personal combinations of theology drawn from a smattering of world religions such as Christianity, Buddhism, Judaism, Hinduism, and Islam as well as secularism."

OUR DESIGNER AND CREATOR

Many people around the world claim to have no belief in the existence of God. Still others believe in God, yet they do not accept Jesus Christ, Yeshua of Nazareth, as their Savior.

Some choose atheism because they are not willing to accept the fact that, as created beings, we must abide by rules of a Creator. I believe that some reject Christ because they lack the information as to what true Christianity really is. Secularists, with their theories of chance origin, will do everything possible to prevent them from finding out.

> ***"How then shall they call on him in whom they have not believed? and how shall they believe in him of whom they have not heard? and how shall they hear without a preacher?"***
>
> ***—Romans 10:14***

Evolutionists may claim that those who believe in the literal words of scripture are ignorant—uneducated in the field of science. That is simply not the case. Creationists have studied evolutionary theory even more closely and recognize the scientific impossibilities associated with chance origins.

If the theory of evolution is mathematically improbable, then one possibility shines through: *"In the beginning, God created the heaven and the earth."*

CORNERSTONE OF THE FOUNDATION

The first verse of the Bible is the foundation upon which all other scriptures are laid. Yet, many do not stand on that foundation, claiming that in the beginning there was nothing but a chance explosion.

> ***"They know not, neither will they understand; they walk on in darkness: all the foundations of the earth are out of course." —Psalm 82:5***

Who are we?
What is our foundation?
Who is the Cornerstone of that foundation?

> ***"Now therefore ye are ...fellowcitizens with the saints, and of the household of God; And are built upon the foundation of the apostles and prophets, Jesus Christ himself being the chief corner stone" —Ephesians 2:19-20***

Today, those who deny the words of scripture attempt to lead us away from the Creator. Setting aside the Cornerstone, Jesus Christ, they attempt to build upon a foundation that will not stand in the day of judgment.

"By the name of Jesus Christ of Nazareth...This is the stone which was set at nought of you builders, which is become the head of the corner. Neither is there salvation in any other." —Acts 4:10

The ever-changing theories of man will one day crumble, for they are built upon a foundation of shifting sand:

"Nevertheless the foundation of God standeth sure, having this seal, The Lord knoweth them that are his."

—2 Timothy 2:19

I'm David Rives,
Truly, The Heavens Declare the Glory of God

About the Author:
Author, lecturer, and singer/songwriter David Rives is known for his presentations "The Heavens Declare the Glory of God" and "Bible Knows Best".

David makes bold assertions and fortifies them with empirical scientific findings...from our own planet Earth to the furthest visible corners of heavens.

With a dozen trips to the Holy Land, David has played a valuable role in historical and archaeological research projects. He has been featured on the History Channel, hosts "Creation in the 21st Century" each week on TBN, seen around the world, and has reached millions by way of his dynamic speaking style, video commentaries, and email newsletters.

About David Rives Ministries:
Through Biblical astronomy, empirical science, the Gospel message, and song, David Rives Ministries shares the majesty of our vast universe and our Creator.

David Rives Ministries' 2007 documentary "The Heavens Declare the Glory of God" has been translated into numerous languages and broadcast on television worldwide. Our 2012 documentary "In The Beginning – Creation According to Genesis" was selected and honored as semi-finalist in the SAICFF, the largest Christian Film Festival in the world.

David gives thanks unto the Lord through his music albums "Forever" and "Fall Down". His comical music video "The Evolution Song" is reaching children in a refreshing way, exposing the ridiculous nature of many of the theories of evolution.

Through national lectures on Creation science and astronomy, David Rives Ministries provides a unique and multi-faceted program that leaves audiences in awe of the Glory of God. A diverse and spiritually inspiring program unlike anything that you have ever seen before. *Exploring the World - Exploring the Universe - and Praising the Creator.*

For booking, contact 931-212-7990 or booking@davidrives.com
For more information, visit our website at:
www.davidrives.com

- In The Beginning - Creation According to Genesis DVD

This concise and to-the-point 30 Minute DVD video is packed with information. David Rives covers a wide array of topics relating to the account of Creation as found in the Biblical book of Genesis (*The Book of Beginnings*).

In 2013, this documentary placed as semi-finalist in the SAICFF, the largest Christian Film Festival in the world. Exposing the various false interpretations of what is written in the Bible, it equips the viewer with the adequate tools needed to understand and share the plain truths of scripture.

If you are looking for an easy-to-understand, visual tool to share, then this DVD is what you have been looking for.

"EVERY WORD OF GOD IS PURE"
HIS WORD IS TRUE... FROM THE BEGINNING

- Wonders Without Number - Book

The book you are holding can be a great resource to introduce friends and family to these topics.

Consider donating a copy to your local library or for your church.

Purchase one as a gift for your pastor.

To learn more and order, visit the David Rives Ministries store:

www.CreationSuperstore.com

You can also order by phone at: (931)212-7990

The Heavens Declare The Glory of God

The original documentary from David Rives Ministries, offering a compelling look at Astronomy from a Creationist's view. This educational DVD provides you with a firm Biblical foundation to stand upon as we are continually faced with lies concerning the true origin of our incredible universe. Since 2007, it has been translated into numerous languages and been broadcast on television worldwide. Did what we see around us just 'happen,' or is there order in the Universe? Learn the answer to this question and many more in this compelling DVD documentary, as you see that truly…

"THE HEAVENS DECLARE
THE GLORY OF GOD"

The Evolution Song Music Video DVD

Today, everywhere we turn, we are bombarded with the theories of evolution. Whether from schoolbooks or educational television, our children are being taught that they are nothing more than apes.

While this is a very serious issue, an entertaining use of comedy and music sometimes relays the ridiculous nature of these theories the best. Join David in this short music video, as he sings "The Evolution Song". You will laugh out loud as he exposes evolution and its error. Great for ages 5 to adult.

Would you believe I'd started out as just a glob of goo?
And changed from fish to bird to ape, and ended up as you?

Evolution – The science of confusion,
Because of all the missing links they don't know what to do.
Evolution – Incredible delusion!
They tell us that we started out as just a glob of goo.

Wonders Without Number DVD - The Six Days of Genesis

Join David Rives and Paul Taylor as they explore the six days of Genesis.

Is God capable of creating everything in six literal days or did he need billions of years? We need to take a look at the Hebrew word 'yom' or 'day' IN CONTEXT and find out what the Bible really says.

"Forever" Music CD

An accomplished singer and songwriter, David Rives offers praises to the Creator in his debut album.

From the heartfelt title track "Le'olam – Forever" to the powerful "We Come (To Praise the Lord)," and the timeless classic "Sweet By and By," there is something for everyone.

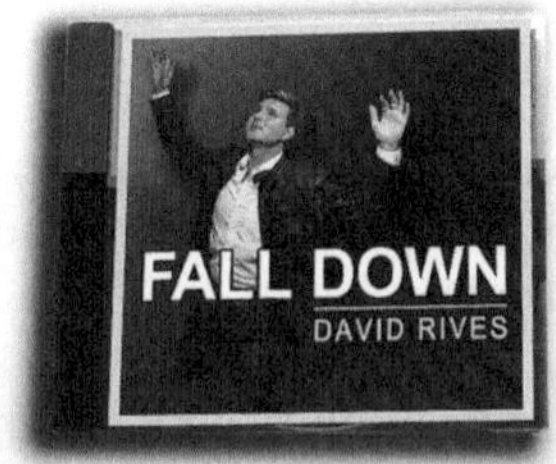

"Fall Down" Music CD

Newest from David Rives Music, comes a powerful EP album. Five inspirational tracks of praise and worship.

THE
CREATION
SUPERSTORE
The Best of Biblical Creation

Visit the Creation Superstore to find all of these resources, plus hundreds of other DVDs and books that relate to Biblical Creation!

www.CreationSuperstore.com

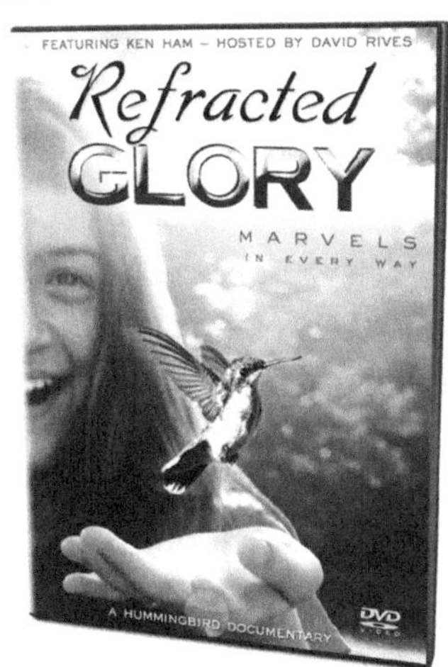

Refracted Glory, Marvels in Every Way - A Hummingbird Documentary

From ancient legends to modern marvels not fully understood, "Refracted Glory" dives into the centuries of intrigue surrounding hummingbirds. David Rives navigates multiple areas of inquiry through captivating interviews with leading experts.

Watch amazing slow-motion footage of awe-inspiring hummingbirds, filmed exclusively for this documentary. Explore the physics of hovering flight alongside scientists, pilots and engineers. Learn about hummingbird biology – and what it means to find fossils in Europe. Two composers worked together to create the musical backdrop for "Refracted Glory" — an original score as dynamic as hummingbirds themselves.

Note from David:
I was approached by Benjamin Owen, an award-winning filmmaker about hosting a feature length documentary on Hummingbirds. As I began to do some preliminary research for the project, I realized that there has never been a documentary made about hummingbirds from a "design" perspective. These incredible creatures are so tiny, yet their capabilities are truly marvelous in every way!

The films in the past that have aired on PBS and nature channels have been consistently from an evolutionary perspective, assuming that hummingbirds arose by means of natural selection over millions upon millions of years. This film "Refracted Glory" is not only inspirational and educational, but NOTHING LIKE IT HAS EVER BEEN PRODUCED... Until now!

Join me on this journey of discovery by ordering your copy today.

Call 931-212-7990 or visit the davidrives.com
"Creation Superstore"

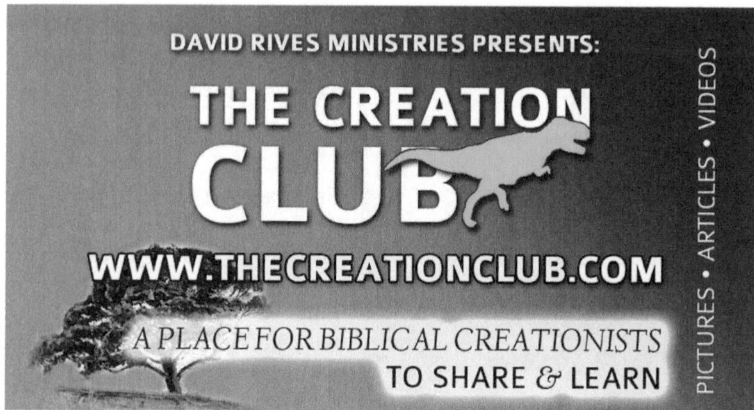

Want to learn more about creation? Have children or grandchildren? Do you use a homeschool curriculum? Learn and be inspired! Visit the Creation Club! Have you written creation-themed articles? Do you take nature photography? Share it with the world on the Creation Club!

A platform for Biblical creationists with weekly columns, hundreds of articles, videos, photo galleries, and more.
www.thecreationclub.com

Creation in the 21st Century with David Rives

Weekly TV show on TBN Featuring interviews each week with leading scientists discussing Creation, Science, and the Bible.

View complete archived programs at:
www.creationinthe21stcentury.com

APPENDIX ONE

STAR CHARTS AND CELESTIAL DATA

THE FOLLOWING PAGES MAY BE OF USE TO THE AMATEUR ASTRONOMY ENTHUSIAST AS A QUICK REFERENCE GUIDE TO THE NIGHT SKY.

SPRING

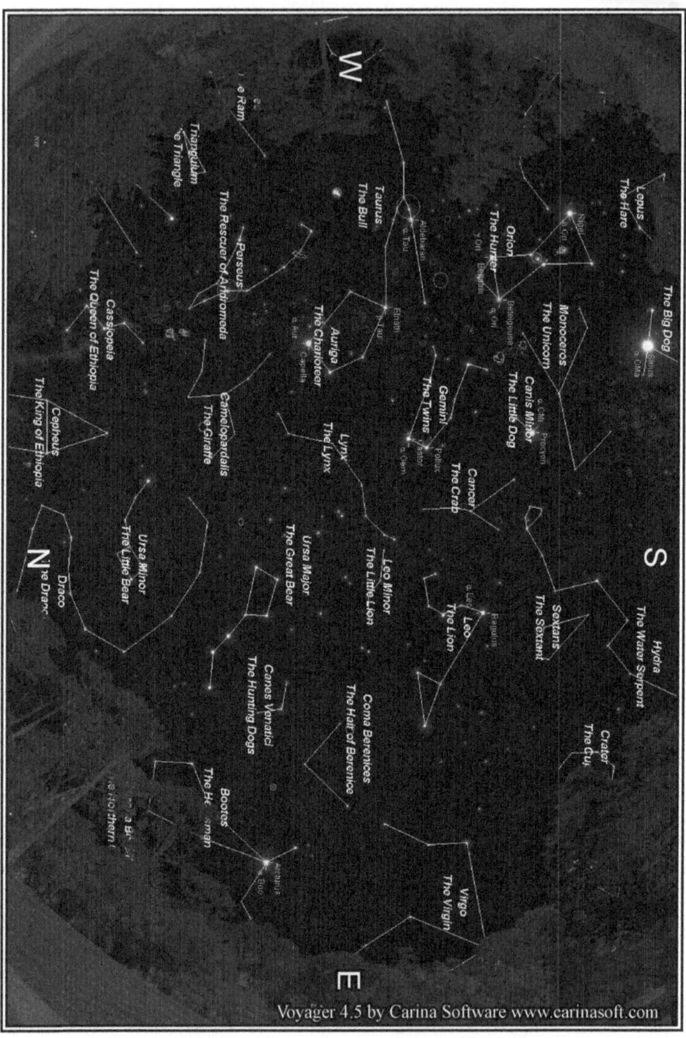

The spring night sky as seen from North America on March 20 at 10:00 PM. Highlights of the spring sky include Ursa Major (containing the Big Dipper), the Pleiades Cluster (close-up on Pg. 164), and the 6th brightest star, Capella.

SUMMER

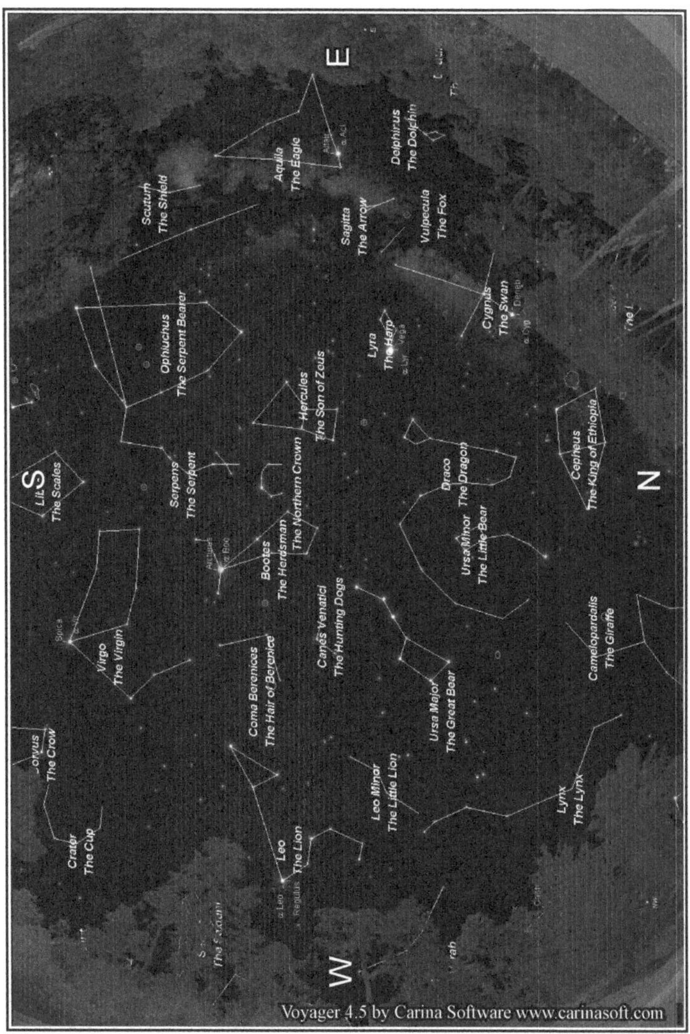

The summer night sky as seen from North America on June 21 at 10:00 PM. Highlights of the summer sky include the constellation Bootes with the 4th brightest star Arcturus marking the tip. This is the perfect time of year to observe the stars and shapes found on Pg. 165.

FALL

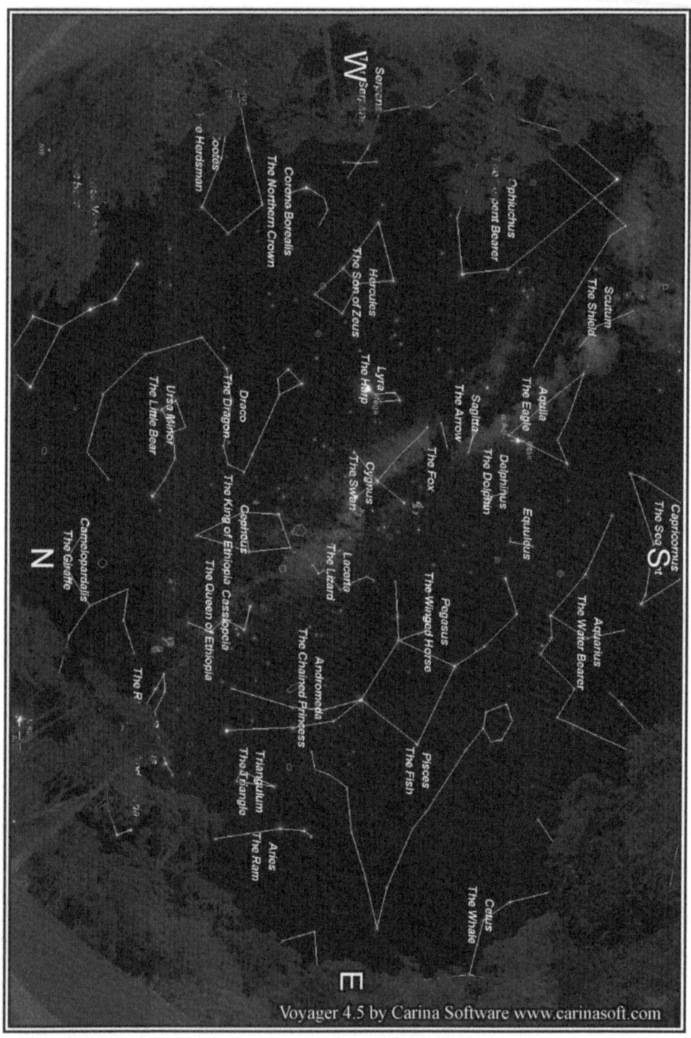

The fall night sky as seen from North America on September 22 at 10:00 PM. Highlights of the fall sky include the constellation Lyra containing the 5th brightest star Vega and the Ring Nebula (Pg. 106). The square shape of Hercules is also easy to find (Pg. 100).

Winter

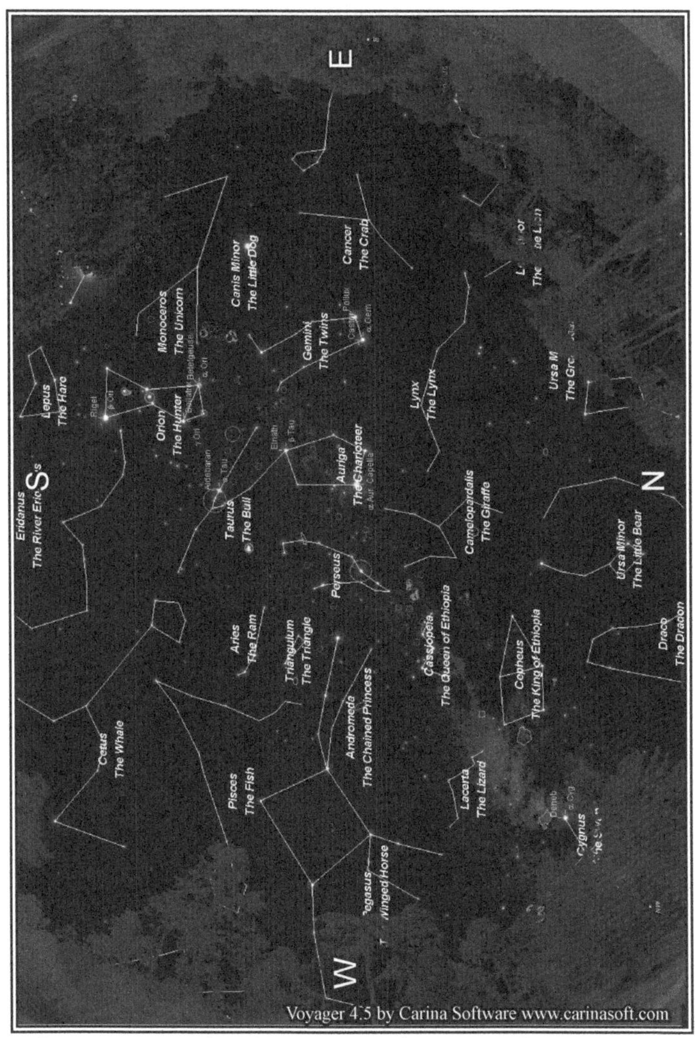

The winter night sky as seen from North America on December 21 at 10:00 PM. Highlights of the winter sky include the constellation Cassiopeia and the nearby Andromeda Galaxy (Pg. 102-103) and spectacular Orion with the Orion Nebula (See Pg. 163, 120-127).

THE CONSTELLATION ORION

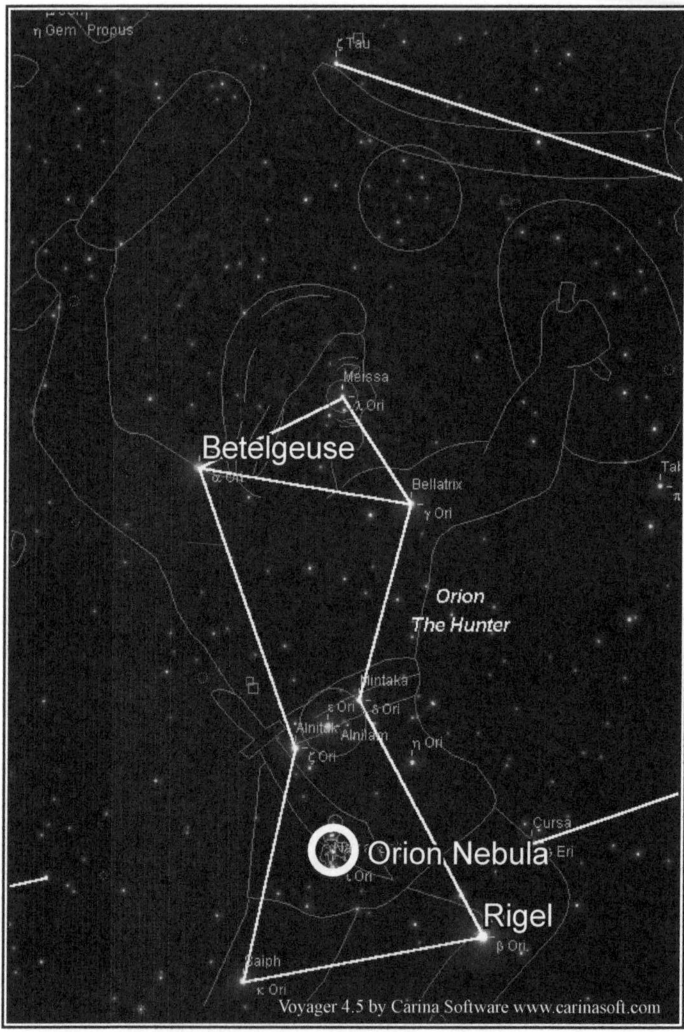

The constellation Orion is one of the most recognized shapes in the Northern Hemisphere. It is easy to spot by the three belt stars along with the stars marking the sword. The Great Orion Nebula is found in the sword. The bright red star Betelgeuse marks the shoulder, while the very bright white star Rigel (3rd brightest), represents the knee or heel. *(See Pg. 120-127 for more information on Orion)*

TAURUS AND THE PLEIADES

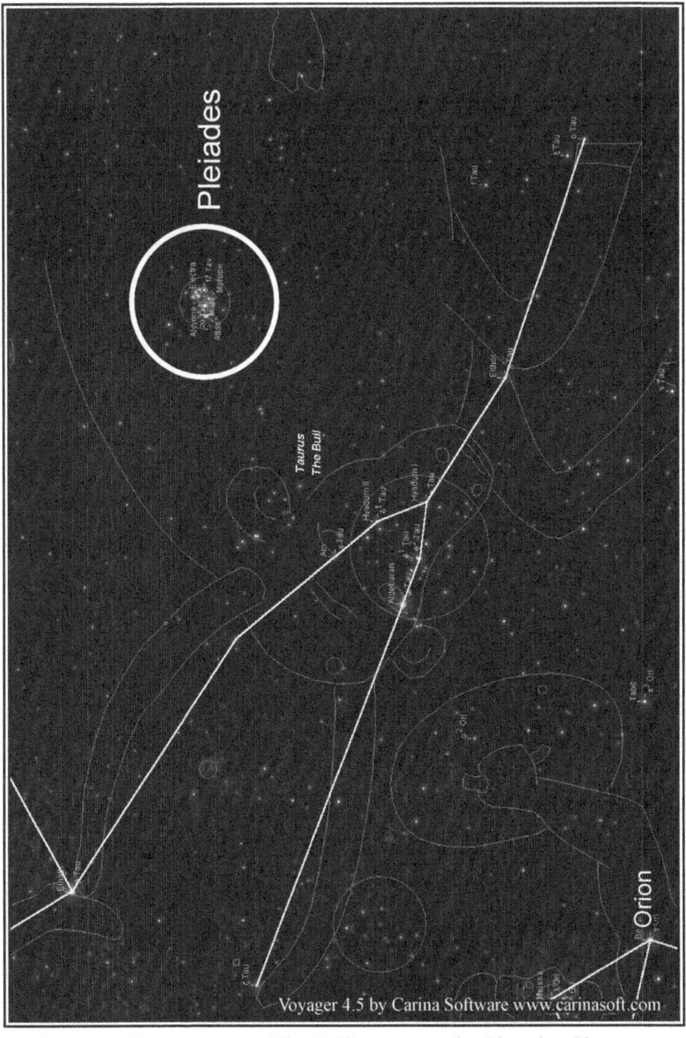

The constellation Taurus (The Bull) contains the Pleiades Cluster or Seven Sisters (See Pg. 127), and the Crab Nebula or M1 (See Pg. 98). Taurus is situated in between the constellations Gemini (The Twins) and Aries (The Ram), and is included in the circle of constellations known today as the Zodiac. The star Aldebaran is the 14th brightest star in the night sky.

ARCTURUS AND SPICA

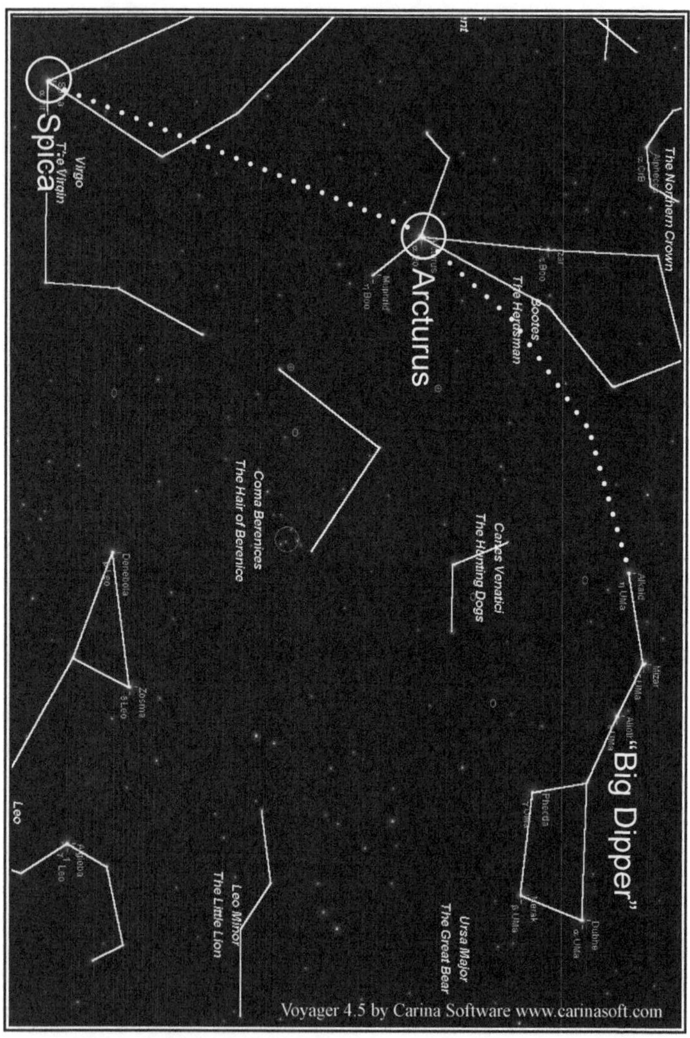

It is easy to find your way around the sky when you know the position of a few easy to find stars. First, spot the "Big Dipper" shape in Ursa Major. Now, following past the curve of the handle, continue to "Arc over to Arcturus". In the constellation Bootes, Arcturus is easy to spot, as it is the 4th brightest star in the sky. From there, "Speed on to Spica" (the 15th brightest star), in the constellation Virgo.

Our Solar System

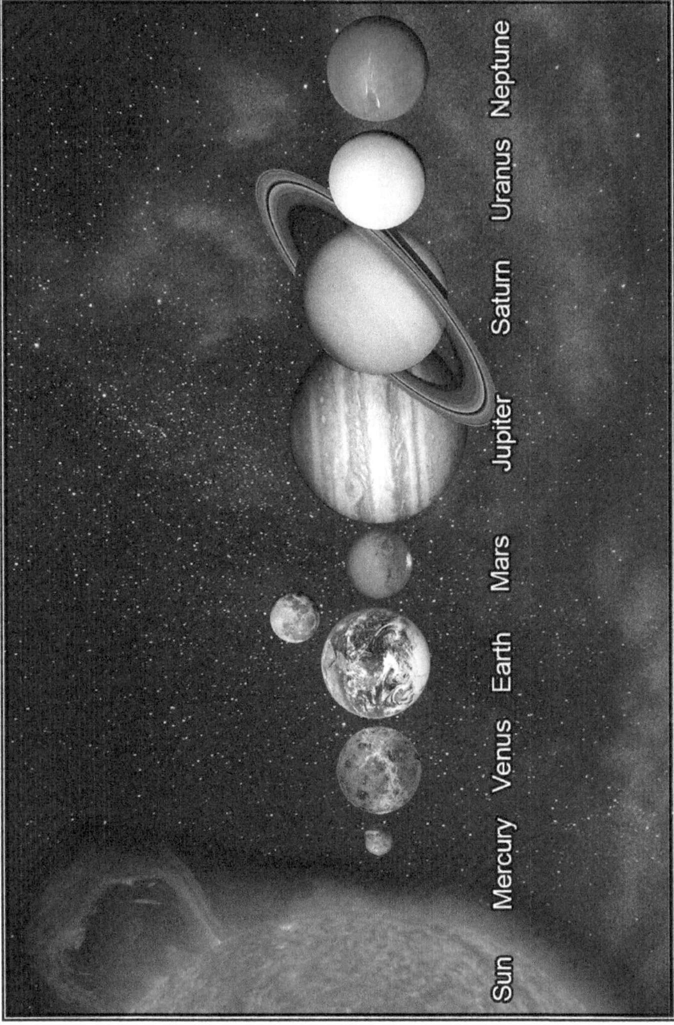

The planets are not to scale, neither are the distances between planets to scale. This composite image shows the order of the planets in relation to the Sun. Pluto is not included, as it was classified in 2006 as a dwarf planet. While the satellites of other planets are omitted, Earth's satellite, the Moon, is included in this representation.

Phases of the Moon

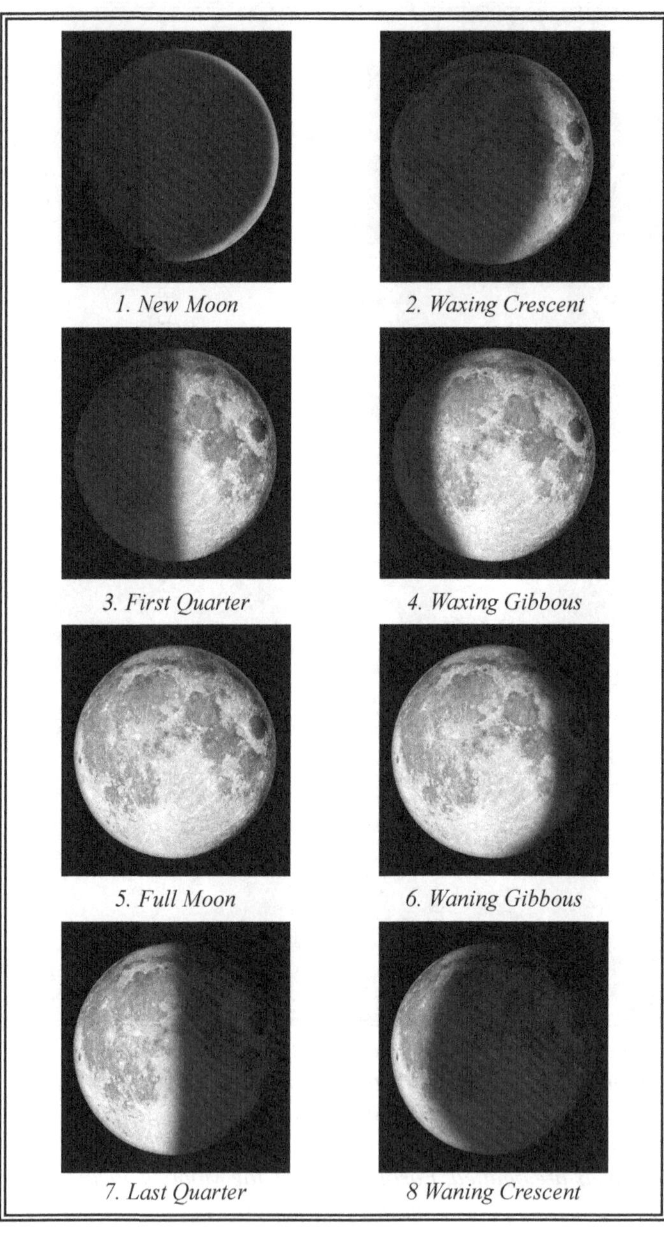

1. New Moon
2. Waxing Crescent
3. First Quarter
4. Waxing Gibbous
5. Full Moon
6. Waning Gibbous
7. Last Quarter
8 Waning Crescent

Surface of the Moon

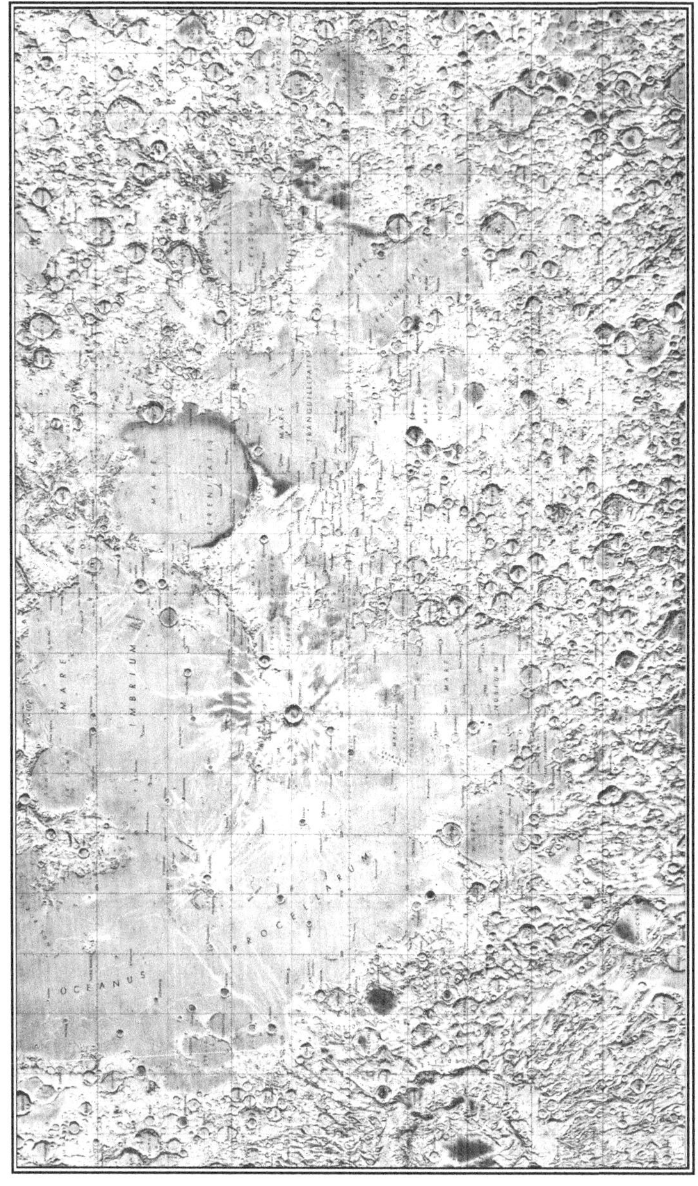

Apparent Star Brightness (Magnitude)

00.	Our Sun	-26.74
01. alpha CMa	Sirius	-1.46
02. alpha Car	Canopus	-0.72
03. alpha Cen	Rigil Kent (A&B)	-0.29
04. alpha Boo	Arcturus	-0.04
05. alpha Lyr	Vega	0.03
06. alpha Aur	Capella (Binary)	0.08
07. beta Ori	Rigel	0.12
08. alpha CMi	Procyon	0.38
09. alpha Eri	Archenar	0.46
10. beta Cen	Hadar	0.61
11. alpha Ori	Betelgeuse	0.70
12. alpha Aql	Altair	0.77
13. alpha Cru	Acrux (A&B)	0.77
14. alpha Tau	Aldebaran	0.85
15. alpha Sco	Antares	0.96
16. alpha Vir	Spica (Binary)	1.04
17. beta Gem	Pollux	1.14
18. alpha PsA	Fomalhaut	1.16
19. alpha Cyg	Deneb	1.25
20. beta Cru	Mimosa	1.25

Apparent Magnitude of Stars from Earth.

The lower the numbers, the more apparent is the brightness. Negative numbers appear very bright, with our Sun at around -26.74. When a system of close stars (binaries, close companions, etc.) appear as one star to the naked eye, the apparent magnitude of the system is measured. Variable stars such as Betelgeuse or Antares may change positions on a brightness chart over time.

Rives' Theory Of Relativity - Distances

Distant Object	Time in Years* (See Description)
Moon	6 Hours
Our Sun	97 Days
Diameter of Solar System	16
Proxima Centauri (Our Closest Star)	70,000
Pleiades	6,999,720
Betelgeuse	10,716,238
The Great Orion Nebula	22,399,104
Ring Nebula	38,331,800
Crab Nebula	108,329,000
Eagle Nebula	116,662,000
Hercules Star Cluster	369,985,200
Andromeda Galaxy	42,331,640,000
Whirlpool Galaxy	383,318,000,000
Sombrero Galaxy	488,313,800,000
Farthest currently observed galaxies	216 Trillion

As outlined earlier in the book, using the Rives Theory of Relativity, we can determine how long it would take us to reach distant stars and galaxies traveling at the speed of our fastest current spacecraft (40,000 MPH) (See Pg. 91 for more information)

**Using our best science to measure distance, (the farther the distance, the more difficult to calculate accurately using most methods) the right column represents the approximate number of years required to reach each object from Earth. When time is less than one year, "Hours" or "Days" will be specified.*

APPENDIX TWO
Dr. Wernher von Braun

The following are several insightful quotes from Wernher von Braun, Director of NASA's Marshall Space Flight Center in Huntsville, AL, and recipient of the National Medal of Science.

> "The two most powerful forces shaping our civilization today are science and religion. Through science man strives to learn more of the mysteries of creation. Through religion he seeks to know the creator.
>
> Neither operates independently. It is as difficult for me to understand a scientist who does not acknowledge the presence of a superior rationality behind the existence of the universe as it is to comprehend a theologian who would deny the advances of science. Far from being independent or opposing forces, science and religion are sisters. Both seek a better world. While science seeks control over the forces of nature around us, religion controls the forces of nature within us.
>
> As we learn more and more about nature, we become more deeply impressed and humbled by its orderliness and unerring perfection. Our expanding knowledge of the laws of the universe have enabled us to send men out of their natural environment into the strange new environment of space, and return them safely to earth.

Since we first began the exploration of space through rocketry, we have regularly received letters expressing concern over what the writers call our "tampering" with God's creation. Some writers view with dismay the possibility of upsetting the delicate balance of the tremendous forces of nature that permit life on our globe.

One letter revealed an honest fear that a rocket would strike an angel in space high above the earth. And one of the Russian cosmonauts stated flatly after his earth-circling flight in space: "I was looking around attentively all day during my flight, but I didn't find anybody there – neither angels nor God..."

Such shallow thinking is childish and pathetic. I have no fear that a physical object will harm any spiritual entities. Manned space flight is an amazing achievement. But it has opened for us thus far only a tiny door for viewing the awesome reaches of space. Our outlook through this peephole at the vast mysteries of the universe only confirms our belief in the certainty of its creator.

Finite man cannot comprehend an omnipresent, omniscient, omnipotent, and infinite God. Any effort to visualize God, to reduce him to our comprehension, to describe him in our language, beggars his greatness. I find it best through faith to accept God as an intelligent will, perfect in goodness, revealing himself in the world of experience more fully down through the ages, as man's capacity for understanding grows. For spiritual comfort I find assurance in the concept of the fatherhood of God. For ethical guidance I rely on the corollary concept of the brotherhood of man. Scientists now believe that in nature, matter is never destroyed. Not even the tiniest particle can disappear without a trace. Nature does not know extinction—only transformation. Would God have less regard for his masterpiece of creation, the human soul?

Each person receives a gift of life on this earth. A belief in the continuity of spiritual existence, after the comparative mere flick of three score and ten years of physical life here in the endless cycle of eternity, makes the action of each moment like an investment with far-reaching dividends. The knowledge that man can choose between good and evil should draw him closer to his creator. Next, the realization should dawn that his survival here and hereafter depends on his adherence to the spiritual rather than the scientific.

Our decisions undeniably influence the course of future events. Nature around us still harbors more unsolved than solved mysteries. But science has mastered enough of these forces to usher in a golden age for all mankind, if this power is used for good—or to destroy us, if evil triumphs. The ethical guidelines of religion are the bonds that can hold our civilization together. Without them man can never attain that cherished goal of lasting peace with himself, his God, and his fellowman."

Dr. Wernher von Braun wrote the following letter regarding the California School Board's debate on the teaching of evolution. It was read by Dr. John Ford to the California State Board of Education on September 14, 1972.

> Dear Mr. Grose: In response to your inquiry about my personal views concerning the "Case for DESIGN" as a viable scientific theory or the origin of the universe, life and man, I am pleased to make the following observations.
>
> For me, the idea of a creation is not conceivable without evoking the necessity of design. One cannot be exposed to the law and order of the universe without concluding that there must be design and purpose behind it all. In the world round us, we can behold the obvious manifestations of an ordered, structured plan or design. We can see the will of the species to live and propagate. And we are humbled by the powerful forces at work on a galactic scale, and the purposeful orderliness of nature that endows a tiny and ungainly seed with the ability to develop into a beautiful flower. The better we understand the intricacies of the universe and all harbors, the more reason we have found to marvel at the inherent design upon which it is based.
>
> While the admission of a design for the universe ultimately raises the question of a Designer (a subject outside of science), the scientific method does not allow us to exclude data which lead to the conclusion that the universe, life and man are based on design.

To be forced to believe only one conclusion—that everything in the universe happened by chance—would violate the very objectivity of science itself. Certainly there are those who argue that the universe evolved out of a random process, but what random process could produce the brain of a man or the system or the human eye?

Some people say that science has been unable to prove the existence of a Designer. They admit that many of the miracles in the world around us are hard to understand, and they do not deny that the universe, as modern science sees it, is indeed a far more wondrous thing than the creation medieval man could perceive. But they still maintain that since science has provided us with so many answers the day will soon arrive when we will be able to understand even the creation of the fundamental laws of nature without a Divine intent. They challenge science to prove the existence of God. But must we really light a candle to see the sun?

Many men who are intelligent and of good faith say they cannot visualize a Designer. Well, can a physicist visualize an electron? The electron is materially inconceivable and yet it is so perfectly known through its effects that we use it to illuminate our cities, guide our airlines through the night skies and take the most accurate measurements. What strange rationale makes some physicists accept the inconceivable electrons as real while refusing to accept the reality of a Designer on the ground that they cannot conceive Him? I am afraid that, although they really do not understand the electron either, they are ready to accept it because they managed to produce a rather clumsy mechanical model of it borrowed from rather limited experience in other fields, but they would not know how to begin building a model of God.

I have discussed the aspect of a Designer at some length because it might be that the primary resistance to acknowledging the "Case for Design" as a viable scientific alternative to the current "Case for Chance" lies in the inconceivability, in some scientists' minds, of a Designer. The inconceivability of some ultimate issue (which will always lie outside scientific resolution) should not be allowed to rule out any theory that explains the interrelationship of observed data and is useful for prediction.

We in NASA were often asked what the real reason was for the amazing string of successes we had with our Apollo flights to the Moon. I think the only honest answer we could give was that we tried to never overlook anything. It is in that same sense of scientific honesty that I endorse the presentation of alternative theories for the origin of the universe, life and man in the science classroom. It would be an error to overlook the possibility that the universe was planned rather than happened by chance.

With kindest regards.
Sincerely,
Wernher von Braun

INDEX

C

D

E

T

U

CPSIA information can be obtained at www.ICGtesting.com
Printed in the USA
LVOW01s0859220315

431345LV00002B/3/P

9 780985 792633